College Is Yours
3

LIVE YOUR LIFE
APPLY TO COLLEGE
NO NEED TO FREAK

PATRICK J. O'CONNOR, PH.D.

outskirts
press

Dedication

He went to Africa as a grieving computer executive and came back as an international hero, feeding the bodies of thousands of children daily, and feeding the souls of hundreds of children as a brilliant college counselor.

For Steve

Table of Contents

Acknowledgments

To my colleagues far and wide, who have cheered me on, nurtured me, nudged me, put up with me, demanded I do better, celebrated when I did, and understood when I didn't. Special thanks to Ken Anselment, Bob Bardwell, Ray Brown, Eva Dodds, Deren Finks, Dave Frick, Holly Markiecki Bennetts, Jessica Fowle, Lucas Inman, Jamie Jacobs, Steve Peifer, Rob Springall, Sarah Summerhill, Julia Varriale, and the CK Dream Team for all you've done to help my students, and move the profession forward.

To Bonnie Schemm, who has worked with College is Yours since it was just an idea. Her creativity, good humor, and determination to make deadlines work, no matter what, have taken CIY to levels that were never expected.

To Ila O'Connor, for thoughtfully proofreading all the *College is Yours* editions, and for being an inspiration.

To Dianne O'Connor, who loves children with every fiber of her being and, by doing so, keeps my work and my writing inspired and grounded.

I

To Gene Kalb and Karen Cotton, who graciously and patiently support the refining of my craft in *High School Counselor Week.*

To Ken Anselment and Julie Gillikin, who utzed me on to write this.

To Randall Dunn, who supported the College is Yours idea at a crucial time.

To Michelle Stamler, for the author's photograph.

To Elaine, Tina, and the entire team at Outskirts Press, for helping so many students make strong college choices.

The Dance of Applying to College

I've never understood why students get so nervous about applying to college. I'm not talking about searching for a college; I'm talking about filling out the actual form. Students learn about all kinds of colleges, work hard to get good grades, do great things outside the classroom, take the right tests—everything we're going to talk about in this book. Then, it's showtime, time to fill out the application and have all that work pay off.

And they freeze. They just can't fill out the form.

I know there's a lot riding on a college application, so students worry that one small mistake could be seen as a deal breaker. But that's pretty hard to do with most college applications, and when it does occur, those mistakes can be pretty easy to fix.

Don't believe me? OK, try this. Pull up the online application for your local community college. If you don't have one, try looking up

Montcalm Community College's online application—it's pretty easy to find.

Got an application on your computer now? Great. Fill it out, then come back here. You don't have to submit it and probably shouldn't, but either way, fill it out. I'll wait.

Seriously. Go.

It's likely been about twenty minutes, and you've applied to college. Congratulations! Chances are, you didn't have to look up anything, you knew all the answers right away, and you didn't need to contact anyone for help. Not such a mystery after all, is it?

I know, I know. You're pretty sure not all college applications are this easy to complete—in fact, you *know* the application for the school you love wants essays, maybe even letters of recommendation from a teacher or two. Much more complicated.

Really? Tell me, have you ever written an essay before? A little bit of work, sure, but once you know the topic, is it really hard to do?

And teacher letters? You know teachers, right? And some of them know you? Well, they know how to write, too, so it's really just a question of asking them on time.

This is sounding a little more doable, isn't it?

It turns out that filling out a college application is kind of like getting ready for prom, or some other school dance. There are a few things you have to do to get ready, and some take more time than others. But once you know what needs to be done, it's more about making the time to do them than anything else.

Still doubt me? Go back to the application you just submitted. What was the first question?

Right. "Name."

Trust me, you can do this. In fact, you just did.

A college application is just filling out a piece of paper, or its online equivalent. The college application process is the application of everything you understand you are into the exploration of what's next for you. It turns out, you can do both with ease. Let's go.

(By the way, I'm not kidding about fixing mistakes on college applications. One student submitted an application with someone else's name on it—his mother's! They called the college, and everything was fine.)

CHAPTER 1

Why College?

For a long time, most students never really thought about why they were going to college—they either did or they didn't. This depended a lot on if you went to a high school where a lot of people went to college. If college was the thing to do, everyone found one and went.

That's changed a little, thanks to two things. First, the cost of college has soared in the last fifteen years to the point where some parents who went to college can't afford to send their own children without some kind of help. Since asking for financial help is something most people are bad at, and getting help is no picnic, many parents are taking the option of college off the table without much discussion.

The second reason is the COVID-19 quarantine. Colleges responded to the initial quarantine in pretty much the same way—by sending everyone home and putting classes online. Since then, colleges have found all kinds of approaches to keeping their students educated and safe, but some of them still don't involve the social parts of college life like they used to, even though the COVID scare is in the rear view mirror.

If you put these two factors together, you can see why some students aren't quite sure if college is what it used to be, and why some parents are wondering what exactly they're paying for. If being a student means staying at home—or worse, being confined to your dorm room—to learn classes online, aren't there less expensive options to do this? On the other hand, if you decide to pass on college, is the economy really going to give you a chance at getting a reasonable job with a high school diploma? Even if that job exists, how safe is it to go out there every day?

The long-term benefits of college are clear. Workers with a four-year degree will likely earn an additional million dollars over their careers, according to some studies, and other studies suggest students who earn a degree are happier people and more engaged in their lives. But all of these findings reflect a college experience that doesn't exist for most people in an economy that isn't likely to be the same anytime soon.

What's the best way to handle this? First, look into the college option with all your heart and soul, as if COVID never existed. Each college still has qualities that make it different and special, and learning about those is a big part of the college search. It's also the only way you can start to figure out where you would feel challenged, supported, and at home—the Big Three of the college search.

Once you've done that, get a feel for what's going on now with the colleges you love. How are classes meeting? Has living on campus gone back to "normal"? Colleges are going to spend the next few years needing more students, so your chances of admission are, in general, better than ever. That means you can afford to ask more questions, to make sure the fit is right between you and the college. That includes cost, and colleges are eager to talk about how to make going there fit your budget.

Money and COVID have changed the way to look at college, but it's still a pretty incredible experience. Before you decide to take a pass, make sure you know what you would be missing out on. What you find will likely surprise you.

CHAPTER 2

What Colleges Are "Looking For"

If your parents went to college, chances are they have already told you applying to college was easy when they were young. According to them, they got up early one Saturday morning, took a test they'd never heard of, applied to a couple of colleges their friends also applied to, and that was it. Simple.

Fast-forward to today. Your friends are freaking out about college, so much so that some aren't telling you where they're applying because they're worried you would take "their" spot. Your phone opens to a "vocabulary word of the day" site, and even your parents—the ones who told you how easy it was for them to apply to college—made you volunteer at a soup kitchen when you were six, since that's "what colleges are 'looking for'."

To those of you who want your choice to be as easy as your parents' choice was, and to those of you who see college applications in your sleep, let me tell you what colleges are really looking for:

4

Live as rich and full a life as you possibly can, and apply only to colleges you love.

Colleges want students who get up every day and give it their all, who go to high schools with limited course offerings and blaze new trails in learning that turn teachers' heads, or who go to fancy high schools and squeeze every drop out of every challenging class. They want students who have taken on a problem, made it their own, and came up with a solution that made someone go "wow." They want students who flew halfway across the world—or just across the street—and gave their hands, hearts, and minds to people they will never see again. They want students who see what is and make it better, different, and more inclusive, which means they change what *is* into what *could be*.

In other words, they want students who, at some level, really *do*.

To those of you who see college as a checklist of doing the "right" things, it's time to reassess. Colleges don't want students who lean on some predetermined recipe that promises college success. Sure, they take those students all the time, but they are the second choice. Colleges will take students who let their lights shine over trained pigeons every day, but the real doers are few and far between. And if you think this is about grades, test scores, and awards, think again. This is about doing everything you can with what you're given—and if you think the folks who run college admissions offices can't tell the difference, you are vastly underestimating the intelligence of these folks.

At the same time, those of you who are hoping that everything will just "work out," it's time to step things up a little. The college you're dreaming of could be the place for you, but if the best reason you can come up with for going there is "Why not?" it's time to find your real purpose for learning and living. You don't have to be a fully grown adult to get into college, but knowing more than a little about who you are and what matters to you in this world helps a lot, both in applying to college and in completing college once you're there.

It would be easy to believe that the key to college is training, or some tried-and-true recipe; that would be a reason to be so busy with essay coaching and such that you wouldn't have time to think about what you're doing. It's also easy to believe that your dream school will beg you to go there and will meet all your needs, unless you haven't been awake enough to know what your needs are. Like most of life, there's a better way to think about college: be you, give it your all, and keep your eyes open every step of the way.

CHAPTER 3

College and Ninth Grade

I have to admit, I'm not crazy about talking college to ninth graders. No matter what I say, these discussions almost always end up centering on test scores and essays—and ninth grade just isn't the time to worry about either. Promise me you won't be thinking about these things, and let's focus on what you can work on—being a great person.

As far as colleges are concerned, there are three things to focus on in ninth grade, and all of them have something to do with being more of who you are. The first one is grades. College is a lot of things—the place where the football stadium is, the home of spring break, and more—but first and foremost, it's a place where academic learning occurs, and that happens in your classes.

One of the best ways to prepare for college classes is to learn as much as you can in the classes you take in high school and be the best student you can be. Unless we're talking art or music school, your admission to college usually depends most on being a good student in challenging classes in high school—not just in eleventh grade, but starting now. Not everyone can do this all the time—in fact, very few people can—but the closer you get to doing your best in every class, every day, the more choices you'll have when it comes time to pick a college. And keeping your options open is what being ready for college is all about.

It's likely you're giving me what you think is a well-deserved eye roll right now. "I need to get good grades? Wow, that is some counseling."

Fair enough, but I didn't say you needed to get good grades. I said you needed to be a good student.

That may sound weird, but colleges get tons of applications from students with great grades who don't know anything. Sure, they got a hatful of As, but the essay asking them to describe a favorite class only shows they were glad the course didn't have many tests. Other students take an approach where they sit in the back of the room, study hard, get an A on the exam, and then do a memory dump. That too shows up in college essays; it also shows up in the teacher letters these students get, where the teachers can say the student got great grades, but that's about it.

That's where becoming a good student comes in. If your math teacher assigns fifteen problems for homework, do the last three in the book that they didn't assign—those are the three that require you to think, not just solve. If your English teacher assigns fifteen pages of reading, take notes as you go. This will require reading, stopping, thinking, and writing, but you can do all these things. Add to these notes every night, and be the student the teacher can count on to answer the question "How does all this tie together?"

If these last two ideas scare you, you may want to sit down. When your history teacher asks for a 250-word essay, write four hundred to five hundred words—in your own words—after you've compared the information in your textbook with what you've learned from a couple of other sources (and as you write, don't forget the reading-stopping-thinking-writing thing). When you write the essay, write the words "ROUGH DRAFT" in big letters on the top page. Three days before the paper's due, ask your teacher to review it with you. Take notes during your meeting, and use those notes when you write the final draft, which is turned in on time.

This kind of learning helps you connect ideas to each other, to the world, and to the way you see the world—and yes, it's the kind of learning colleges like to see. This may require some changes to your social schedule (there are always study groups!), and it's always a good idea to talk to your teacher about study tips (chances are the study skills guru in your building teaches special education—really). In two or three months, you'll see this is the most important chapter in the book, since it will make you a thinker and a doer who knows how to learn and loves to learn. That gets you halfway into college. More importantly, it gets you most of the way to a great life.

CHAPTER 4

Extracurricular Activities

Learning doesn't occur only in the classroom, and what you do outside the classroom can help you learn more about yourself and the world around you, all while having a pretty good time. Here's what you need to know:

- Extracurriculars can be thought of as hobbies or interests. Sports, clubs, summer classes, travel, work jobs, and internships are the big ones, but they aren't the only ones.
- You want a mix of extracurriculars, both in content and duration. It's great to play sports for four years or have the same job through all of high school, but aim for some variety, too. Trying out new things is a big part of college; let your extracurricular record show that, if you can.
- If you're wondering, no, there is no "magic" list of extracurriculars colleges like to see. You want to choose them based on interest and the time you have to do them while keeping your grades up.
- Don't go crazy. Signing up for seven new clubs in junior year will likely be seen as suspicious by the colleges—like you're trying to pad your application. Don't do it.

- If you have limited time for extracurriculars because you have to work or you have family obligations, make sure to relate that information to your colleges. Work and babysitting offer great life lessons and can easily be seen as a couple of pretty powerful extracurriculars.

- Extracurriculars and community service are two different things, but they can overlap. If your high school basketball team runs the summer league for elementary students, that's an extracurricular *and* community service. Same if the French club visits senior centers. Use some creativity with your leadership skills. That makes for a great life, and a unique application.

- Starting your own club at school is OK, but be careful. Lots of students start a club to show leadership but end up being the only member of the club, which makes them "president"—and suspect in the eyes of the colleges. If you start something, make sure you involve others, make sure it meets often, and make sure you point all of this out to the colleges. This needs to be the real deal.

- Remember that not all extracurriculars happen at school. Your local library, community center, YMCA and YWCA, place of worship—there's a lot out there!

- Work hard, but keep balanced. Some of the students I've worked with only participated in extracurriculars in the summer, so they could focus on their studies. Others knew that they would have to ease up on Spanish Club during basketball season because they didn't have time for both. Balance is the key.

- Be clear and fair. My hometown, Detroit, is about forty-five minutes from Canada, so my students are sometimes tempted to claim they are "international travelers." Um, no. If you went to Canada, tell them that.

- Starting in ninth grade, find a place to write down all you're doing. That can be a notebook, a computer, a special website your school provides for you—whatever works. Just start early; you'll forget half of what you did by the time you apply to college, and it's all important.

Your diet of extracurriculars should be like food at a good Super Bowl party: a great main course or two and really interesting appetizers. Do that, and you'll be ready for college, life, and some awesome tailgate parties.

CHAPTER 5

Community Service

If you have an older brother or sister who applied to college, they are likely to tell you community service is a Really. Big. Deal. At one point, many colleges listed community service separately from extracurricular activities as a way of showing students how important it was to the college.

That doesn't happen as much as it used to, but colleges still care a great deal about community service—and with good reason. A good chunk of the wonderful things that happen on college campuses are done by student volunteers, and students are more likely to be college volunteers if they were high school volunteers. Practice, practice, practice.

There are two kinds of community service. The first is a regular, dedicated volunteer effort on your part to improve conditions in your community that have no direct impact on your life. In other words, you are regularly working at making things better for someone else. Volunteering at a retirement home, soup kitchen, local community center, the Red Cross, a place of worship—you get the idea. Volunteer work at a local business would likely not count—that's more like an internship—and neither does doing chores around your house—that's more like life. Both are important; they just aren't community service.

Some high schools have a community service "requirement" you have to complete in order to graduate. This is a good idea, since it helps show you the importance of helping others, but colleges aren't always crazy about it because it's "volunteer" work you *had* to do, and that's a little confusing. You can, and should, list it on a college application, but make sure you tell them it was required.

Regular, dedicated work means you're volunteering consistently, one to two hours a week or for an intense period of time over the summer, starting in ninth grade. It's important to remember you are doing this because you want the world to be better and are willing to do something about it. The wise people who review college applications can tell if you're just doing this to suck up to them, and that's just awkward, so pick a cause that means something to you and lean into it. Don't let the prospect of another COVID scare, scare you off of community service. There are ways to help others that can be done in safe ways, and the need is great.

The second kind of community service is just as important but less frequent. This is a "roll up your sleeves" kind of community service, where someone needs you to box canned goods for a day, shovel driveways after the big storm, or help your elementary school build a new playground. These are a little harder to tell colleges about, but collectively, they show you're the kind of person who can be counted on to step up.

Either way, be careful about doing "beauty contest" community service, where a company will charge you several thousand dollars to go to a remote country, play with schoolchildren for one afternoon, and then spend five days on vacation. Colleges know about these and can sniff them out in a minute. Real commitment to those in need, through mission work and Habitat for Humanity, is always valued, but be careful not to overlook the needs of your own community.

No matter what you're doing, community service only truly works if you are doing it out of a sense of helping others—neighbors, strangers, or the world. College admissions officers have a way of peering into your heart that might be considered a little scary, except that it's good for us. It makes us keep the bigger picture in mind: that life isn't about glory or recognition. It's about living.

PS, Mom and Dad: If you want to make sure your child's community service commitment gets off to a strong start, find a project all of you can work on together in ninth grade. Nothing like setting the example.

CHAPTER 6

Summer Programs and "You've Been Nominated"

Many students (and parents) spend lots of time looking for the College Admissions X Factor, that extra class, program, or recognition that will, all by itself, guarantee admission to the college of their choice.

Some people believe the answer lies in the "right" summer program, especially the ones offered on college campuses. From writing seminars to business camps to rock band minicourses, these programs offer you a chance to take an established interest to the next level, or try something new, focus on it intensely over the summer, and get a taste of what it's like to live on a college campus on your own.

Those are the best, and only, three reasons to participate in a summer program. Activity outside the classroom expands your view of yourself and the world, things colleges are fond of; but so does working all summer to build up your college fund, reading through *Ulysses* all summer and hosting a blog for like-minded readers, and traveling to the Vietnam Memorial to help your grandmother honor the soldiers she served with.

All of these things can enrich your life and expand your world, but all of them (even summer programs at selective colleges) can also be done mindlessly with a pair of earbuds distracting you from getting the most out of the experience. Part of the experience is what you do, but a bigger part is what you let the experience do to you. Colleges will want to know about both.

This is especially important if you think a summer program at an "elite" college will automatically give you some kind of admissions boost, particularly at that college. Admissions representatives say your participation (even at programs they don't host) will strengthen your application, but one program by itself isn't a sure bet to getting in. In some cases (that's some cases), a letter from a college professor teaching the class can be a boost, but that letter is usually based on one week of interaction, so it has its limits. In addition, many colleges don't even know about the summer programs run on their campus, since many are run by private companies who rent the campus in order to make their program look more select or important.

It's great to want to do more, but do it for the right reason. Summer programs are one way to do this, but only one way. If you go this route, make the most of the program and learn as much as you can. That's the real goal, and one the colleges will notice.

Another "sure thing" people think colleges love are letters telling students they've been "nominated" to attend a summer program, join a select society, or have their names printed in a yearbook with other select students. These invitations almost always involve some kind of fee; those that are free typically "invite" you to buy copies of the yearbook for you, your friends, your parents, and the US Secretary of Education.

Some of these "by invitation" programs are good, but some aren't, and there are likely others that are just as good that cost far less. Either way, none of them give you any more clout in the admissions process than other summer programs. Ask around to see if other students have attended them, check with your school counselor for more affordable opportunities, and proceed with care.

As for the societies (except for National Honor Society) and the yearbooks, forget it. It's usually never clear who "nominated" you, and none of these programs are given any weight by most colleges, who tend to view them as money-making schemes. Some offers may tempt you with a scholarship—that's part of what they do with your "membership fee," and it's almost always won by somebody else.

The pressure to get in the "right" college leads to pressure to find the "right" summer program. You really have to dump that mindset. It's an illusion, and you deserve real answers and real experiences.

CHAPTER 7

Playing the College Admissions "Game"

Most of what you hear about applying for college is wrong. Yes, there are colleges that have so many applications they can only admit less than 10 percent of the applicants—but that's about one percent of all colleges in the country, according to the Pew Foundation. Nearly 80 percent of all colleges admit half their applicants or more. They still want students who have made the most out of high school (and life); it's just that there's much more room for them at most colleges than you might think.

That's important to know because many people who get their college information from the newspapers think it's *soooo* hard to get into college. It's either some kind of random selection process or a game you have to play—doing things you really don't care about just to get in.

Truth is, it doesn't work that way. First, colleges can sort out the truly interested students from the "college is a game" players in a heartbeat. The folks who are trying to look good add a dozen clubs junior year and go to two meetings of each one; the doers are active in a group or two starting in (or even before) ninth grade, contributing two to five hours per week in a cause they believe in. This kind of commitment usually opens up leadership possibilities, but even if it doesn't, you'll have three hundred to seven hundred hours of community service, and lots of great essay possibilities, to tell colleges about—while still having time for studies, families, and a couple of extracurriculars.

Second, just like good study habits, the way you approach school and life improves your learning in a big way. Giving up some of your TV or chat time for the swim team or volunteer work puts you in the center of the real world, where you learn about the give-and-take of life, the differences between people, and the importance of everyone pitching in and doing their best. By giving to the world in and out of the classroom, you are showing an interest in the world and a willingness to challenge yourself. What college doesn't want a student who does that?

Third, doing these things gets you ready for—hang on here—life after college. I know that's a few years and a zillion Friday nights down the road, but it's coming, and you need to be ready. If you can practice juggling school and life now, you'll be a master at juggling work and life when you're twenty-five, and keep at it until you're 125. Imagine a world where everyone knows how to work hard, play hard, and let go. That would be like college forever!

It's usually right here where students tell me, "Right, but I stink at everything." Look, think about the people who go to gyms to work out. The place isn't filled with athletic superstars, just with people who like to work out. Some will be ripped, some will be wearing trendy outfits, and some will struggle to bench press eighty pounds, but they'll all be working at giving their all, trying to make a difference with what they have to give, and loving the challenge they've made for themselves.

And that's the whole idea: Love what you're doing so much that what the person next to you thinks about you is irrelevant. You might not get an award or a team captainship to throw on your college application, but, then again, you might. Either way, you've broken the myth by giving, living, and learning in the real world, not dancing like a puppet, hoping the right college picks you.

In other words, you've won the college game by never playing it.

CHAPTER 8

One Example of What College Ready Looks Like

Sara came home from a softball game and was surprised to see her father's car in the driveway. It was May, and that's a busy time where he works, so he usually went back to the office after he watched her pitch, finished a little paperwork, and then headed home for dinner.

That day, he greeted his daughter in the kitchen. "Nice game, Ace!"

"Thanks, Daddy. Why are you home?"

He beamed at his eleventh grade daughter and said, "I have a surprise. There's an overseas community service project heading to a village in Haiti. They've opened a large orphanage in a remote area, and they need volunteers to watch the babies while the residents rebuild their homes."

Sara peeled an orange while her father continued.

"You'd be there four days, but you'd only be working two. You'd have two more days to sightsee. Your grades are strong and your pitching is great, but I think something like this could put you over the top at the colleges we're applying to. The website for the project is up on your computer. What do you say?"

Sara continued to peel the orange. "Can we talk about it at dinner?"

Her father was a little deflated, but he smiled back. "Sure, honey. I'm going to run back to the office for a little bit, but I'll see you at seven."

Dad came through the kitchen door at 7:15 p.m. and quickly took his place at the table with the rest of the family. After more congratulations for Sara's great game and a little razzing from younger brother John about Sara's hair, her dad said, "So, how about Haiti?"

Sara put her fork down slowly and looked up. "It's a great idea, Dad, but I looked on the website. Does this trip really cost six thousand dollars?"

Her father choked on his ice water while her mother gave him a long, cold stare.

"We can afford this, Sara," he said, smiling faintly. "It's about your future."

Sara looked down at her placemat again and swallowed hard. "Well, I looked up the name of the town we'd be going to. It turns out Habitat for Humanity is working there, too. They need three thousand dollars for a new pump so the town can have fresh water again. I also called the Boys Club down on Wilson Street, and they said they could really use some help this summer.

"I sure appreciate the offer, Daddy, but don't you think it would be better if I stayed here, and we sent three thousand dollars to Habitat for Humanity? That way, the town would have fresh water forever, John could get that new computer he needs, we'd have a little money left over for college, and I would still be making a difference in the world. It would just be a difference in my own neighborhood."

Sara's mother did a very bad job of chewing nonchalantly, and John tried to wipe tears out of his eyes in a fourteen-year-old macho fashion. Her father's shoulders relaxed, and he smiled almost to himself.

"Yeah, honey," he said. "That's a great idea."

Sara is now a senior, waiting to hear from her colleges. But the question you should be asking isn't "Where will she get in?"

The question to consider is, does it really matter?

CHAPTER 9

College Readiness and Tenth Grade

Ninth graders, if your parents are making you read this book, you're done until next year. You have eight chapters of good ideas to put into practice, and that's more than enough for now. Read on if you wish, but if understanding your college readiness duties as ninth graders was the goal, you've made it.

In terms of college, tenth grade starts with the same ground rules as ninth grade. Strong grades in the most challenging classes you can take, commitment to community service, and some solid extracurriculars are the foundation of a strong tenth grade experience. You may discover you're spending more time on homework and studying this year, but that's supposed to happen. The classes are harder.

In addition to building on this strong foundation, there are a couple of other things to add to your college readiness playbook. Chances are your school is going to give you, or offer you, the chance to take a standardized test or two, and one of them is likely to be some kind of variation of the PSAT. The PSAT is designed for juniors to take in the fall, but some schools give it to their tenth graders for practice. That's an interesting choice because there's also a test called the PSAT 10, which is designed to be taken by—well, you get the idea.

Some schools like to challenge their students, so they give everyone the PSAT. No matter what you take, the colleges will never see your scores, and it's always good to understand the way in which the questions are written, so it's worth taking the test.

If you end up taking the PSAT, remember that this test is designed to measure what you know *as a junior*. In many cases, this means your score on the PSAT may not be as high as you'd like it to be, since you may be tested on material you haven't had yet in math or English. This isn't something to panic about; it happens to most students. As long as you know it's coming, you can take the test, do your best, and see what happens.

The other major college test is the ACT, and it too offers a version for tenth graders, the PreACT. Fewer schools offer this test, but if that's available to you, give it a shot. It gives you the same insights into the ACT that the PSAT gives students about the SAT, and much of your success on the tests you take as a junior depends on being familiar with the way the test is structured and how the questions are asked.

If you're worried the PreACT won't prepare you for the SAT, remember that just about every college in the United States that requires or accepts test scores is happy to take either the SAT or the ACT—there are about twelve colleges that have a preference, and none of those recruit students nationally, so this isn't something to worry about. You also want to remember that thousands of colleges no longer require either test. You can submit the scores if you wish, but you don't have to—in some cases, colleges won't look at your scores even if you submit them.

We'll talk more about this later, but the bottom line is if you have a chance to take the PreACT or some version of the PSAT in tenth grade, keep your options open and go for it. If you want to practice, there are all kinds of free practice tests and resources online, and if you require extra time or special accommodations to take your school tests, you can ask for the same for these tests, too. Either way, remember there's nothing at stake here—this is all practice, like band rehearsals or sports workouts.

CHAPTER 10

Getting to Know a College

They're small. They're big. They're in the middle of big cities, where their campus is part of downtown. They're out in remote areas all by themselves, so you can focus on learning and living with your fellow students.

Some offer the chance to study overseas. Some will let you change your major into junior year. Some require you to live on campus every year you study there. Some have no dorms.

You study the menu closely when you go to a restaurant for the first time, so you can make a wise choice. The same is true for choosing a college. It's important to take a look around and see what you can choose from.

It's also important to do this because learning about colleges can bring a bit of a buzz. You're studying hard, you're taking tests, you're putting in long hours—it can be easy to forget what you're doing this for. But then you visit a college campus or do an online chat with an admissions officer, and you're pumped up again. You're ready to go *now*, but since that can't happen, you're ready to prepare for when you can go.

COVID has changed the way many students get to know different colleges. It used to be you would sign up for a campus visit, take the tour, eat lunch in the dining hall, and see the dorms firsthand. If you can still do that safely, do it. Seeing where you will be is the best way to know how it feels, and that's important. Some colleges now offer walking or driving tours you do on your own in the safety of your family. This is also a great option.

If getting to campus simply won't work, don't worry. Colleges get that not all students want to travel, or can travel, to campus—and if some campuses are offering online classes, there's not that much to see anyway. Online tours are available at most of these colleges, and most of those include a Q and A session at the end with students who go there. Since most of these tours are also led by admissions officers, you could have a chance to talk to the person who will be reading your application. Talk about making a strong first impression.

No matter how you build up your college knowledge, you want to put together a starter list. In-person visits can start with colleges close to you. Even if you may not be interested in staying close to home, you can use these visits as practice for when you focus your list as a junior. If you're exploring colleges online, the sky is the limit, and a website like Big Future can help. Be sure to sign up for a tour where you can ask questions, and make sure you sign up in advance. It may sound weird, but some online information sessions have limited enrollment.

There are two key steps to making this research count:

1. Personalize the visit as much as you can. If history is your thing, visit the department if you're on campus, and meet with a professor if you're online. Want to know what the workout facilities look like? Ask to see them. Don't worry if you don't

know what your major is going to be; almost no one does. Just start with the things you feel are important to a good college. If you need help thinking about that, look up Questions to Ask on a Campus Tour. That will get you going.

2. Write down your impressions. You swear you will remember everything about the college you just saw until you see another college, and now you're mixing up the two. Take a moment to write down what you liked, what you weren't crazy about, and what questions you have. You'll thank me for this.

You're making your way to the banquet hall of college. Make sure you know what's on the menu.

CHAPTER 11

Highly Selective Colleges

As you look at colleges, you may be interested in one of the fifty or so colleges that most people talk about. These colleges include those in the Ivy League (which really is just an athletic league) and other schools that get so many applicants, it sometimes seems you have a better chance of getting struck by lightning than you do getting admitted.

It's easy to say admission to these schools is a mix of luck and random selection, but there's a little more to it than that. Most of these schools recruit a large number of athletes, since they tend to have an incredible number of sports teams, given their size (most have about five thousand students). Many of these schools admit a large number of applicants who have relatives who attended the school. Add in any special applicants they need in any given year—a bassoon player, more students from the Midwest—and that small percentage of applicants they admit gets even smaller if you don't play a sport or are not related to someone who went there.

If you're interested in a highly selective college, make sure it's for the right reason. Like any college, these schools offer some great majors, but they also have some clunkers—and some students who go to these schools say many of them are more interested in the graduate students than the undergrads. Just like any other college, get to know the campus and the town, talk to a couple of students who go there, and if you know about a major, talk to professors in the department.

If your research leads you to believe this is a place for you, get ready to dig in. It may seem that these colleges are looking for students who walk on water, but they're really looking for the students who are truly, deeply committed to living and learning. Most successful candidates have taken some or all of the most demanding classes their high school offers, and many have already taken some classes at local colleges. Many of the admitted science majors have already done some kind of research with a medical department or college professor, if that's available. Nearly all have done something to create learning opportunities for themselves and others that stand out from what other students have had in their high school, and often in the state.

Even if you do all these things, that low admit percentage suggests there isn't room for every incredibly committed student at one of these colleges, and that's true. I'm mentioning this now because you don't want to work like crazy in high school, assuming you have an automatic admit to a dream school many other students dream about, too. That's why you can't apply to a highly selective college by padding your application with things that "look good"; this is about enriching your life with activities that deeply interest you. The hours of practice, the TV given up for summer programs, the time away from family—this is way more commitment than giving up a few Saturdays to prepare for the SAT. As one admissions officer put it, you don't have to be perfect to get into these schools, but you do have to demonstrate excellence, often in most everything you do.

It's certainly true that selective colleges take a lot of straight-A students who weren't the ambassador to Spain at age twelve, but if you look closely, you'll see many more students there who have sent the message that they know who they are—and who they are is seriously committed. If that's you, give this goal your all, making sure to also apply to other schools that have the same qualities as the highly selective schools but with slightly more generous admission rates. No one will judge you if you aim for this goal and miss, because aiming the right way means learning about yourself and the world around you at a deep, meaningful level. That's something to respect no matter where you end up going to college.

CHAPTER 12

Talking with Your Parents about College

Now that you're starting to look at colleges, there are a couple of other people who are going to play an important role in what happens to you after high school. Some of those people would be your parents.

I can hear you now.

"No, no. They're just going to mess things up."

I get it. You want this to be a personal experience, something you do for you that's mostly about you. Including others, especially Mom and/ or Dad, could easily lead to a situation where this is more about them than it is about you.

So make sure that doesn't happen.

In addition to being a college counselor, I teach American Government, and one of the important lessons in learning government is to understand that both sides can be right on any given issue. It's the same thing with college; you want some space to make sure the choice you make is right for you. Your parents want to make sure you are safe and have a good future, and that they aren't throwing money away paying for you to go to a college where they care more about football games than they do about classes. Fair enough.

The way you both get what you want is through a weekly meeting. At the beginning of the college selection process, student and parents agree to meet once a week for twenty minutes to talk about college. During these twenty minutes, it's OK to ask any question about college. Your parents can ask if you're taking enough college prep classes, if any colleges are visiting your high school this week, if you made that appointment with your counselor—anything.

The same is true for you. You can ask why you have to apply to the same college they went to, how they would feel if you took a year off before starting college, why they embarrassed you by asking that lame question on the last video tour of a campus—again, anything goes. Nobody loses their cool, nobody interrupts, and everybody ends the meeting knowing what they need to do to answer someone else's questions. Unless the answers are time sensitive, they're shared at next week's meeting, which is the next time anyone gets to talk about college.

This is a time-proven way to talk about college without going crazy. College doesn't become the thing you always talk about, but no one has to wonder how everyone else is feeling about your college plans, either. While there's no hard and fast rule about when to start these meetings, most families begin them sometime during junior year. No matter when you start yours, try to be the first one to propose the weekly meeting. This will give your parents the correct impression that you have your act together and that you care about what they have to say. It will also give you a little breathing room. Once parents know you've got things under control, they're less inclined to clip your wings and more inclined to let you fly.

I've seen a lot of students make great college plans on their own, only to see them disappear because they didn't bring Mom and Dad along for the ride a little at a time. You want to drive the college selection bus, and you should. Having passengers come with you makes for a smoother ride and is usually a lot more fun, especially if they bring food to the meetings.

CHAPTER 13

Working with Your School Counselor

Driving the college bus means taking care of all the passengers, and that includes someone whose role is pretty important—your school counselor.

Go ahead, I'll wait.

"Hang on. So I meet with my parents every week, *and* I have to stay in touch with someone I've only met once when I changed my schedule?"

Exactly right—and that's the problem. If you look at most college applications, there's a section that has to be filled out by your school counselor. It doesn't matter how well the counselor knows you. It doesn't matter how many other students they work with. It doesn't matter how many other things your counselor does besides help students get into college. The colleges want to hear from your counselor.

That means one of three things will happen with the space the counselor has to complete. It stays blank; your counselor scribbles something in it that could apply to anyone; your counselor has so many helpful things to say about you they have to write "continued on attached document."

Two questions here. First, if you gave this form to your counselor today, what option would they choose? Second, which option are you rooting for?

Thought so.

This isn't hard. For the first two years of high school, see your counselor when you need to—when you need to change a schedule, discuss a personal issue, apply for a summer program—and, if they have time, talk about college. Like it or not, your counselor is way overworked—schedule changes, college and career plans, and personal guidance for five hundred students keeps them busy—so the group counseling programs they run and an occasional "hi" from you will go a long way in meeting both your needs. So go see them if you need them; if not, space is good.

In most cases, the time to ramp things up is in February of junior year. If your school is like most, this is when you'll schedule classes for senior year. By the end of January, you'll want to type up a summary of your community service and extracurricular activities, along with any awards and recognitions you've received. Complete this with one to two paragraphs explaining why you want to go to college. This way, the notes or letter your counselor writes for the college will be more than just a list of what you've done; it will show them more of who you are. That makes a difference.

You'll also want to have your senior schedule written up and finished. Your counselor may have scheduled this meeting to talk about your classes, but you don't want to do that. Instead, put all these materials in a folder that has your name on the front. Hand it to your counselor when your meeting starts and then say this:

"Mrs. Jones, I know you're really busy, so I got a copy of my transcript from the office and planned my senior schedule already. I also want you to know I'm scheduled to take the SAT in April, and I'm doing some in-person and online college tours over spring break. I don't know if I'll see you before I apply for colleges in the fall, so here's a list of what I've been up to in high school, along with my thoughts about college. I've highlighted the activities that mean the most to me, and my cell number is at the top of the page, so you can contact me right away if you have any questions. Thanks for helping me with this. If I have any questions, what's the best way to contact you?"

I promise you—if you do this, your counselor will look for reasons to see you from now on, and that's a good thing.

Counselor on board? Drive on.

CHAPTER 14

College Fairs

Another way to explore colleges is to participate in a college fair, which is a great way to learn more about all kinds of colleges and very helpful if you're deciding which college campuses to visit. Typically held in the fall and spring, college fairs can have representatives from up to four hundred colleges, all eager to talk with you about their college and your life. Many fairs feature information sessions on applying to college and for financial aid, and most fairs are free.

The college fair format translated nicely to the internet during the COVID crisis. Each college has its own room within the site, so you can "wander" from one school to the other and stay as long as you like. In many cases, you'll find you're the only one in the room, which means you get a shot at a mini-interview with the college representative, who is often the first person to read your college application.

With so many colleges at a fair, it's easy to be intimidated. Take (or if it's an online fair, have handy) a highlighter, a pen, an unofficial copy of your transcript, and five questions committed to memory that will help you learn more about each college—information you can't get online. What you ask is up to you—majors, food, chances for research, cost, social life—just make sure the answers will help you decide if this place is worth a closer look.

If it's an in-person fair, get a map of where the colleges are located *before* you start meeting colleges. A list of participating colleges is usually on the fair's website, so you can scope this out ahead of time.

With either kind of fair, once you're with a college rep, you might have to wait to answer questions—and that's good! This gives you a chance to listen to what the college rep is saying to other students. Since they will most likely be discussing general questions, you can use your time to ask questions more specific to your interests.

Once it's your turn, get busy. "Hi, my name is (First and last—*No* student does this, which is exactly why you should—it shows confidence and gives the rep something to remember about you), and I go to John Lewis High School." From here, you want to ask your questions. Look the admissions rep in the eye when they answer your question, and don't rush them.

If you feel like things are going well and there's not much of a crowd, pull out your transcript (or share it on your screen) and say, "Just one more question. I'm putting my senior year schedule together. Here's what I've taken so far. What other courses would your college like me to take?" Again, *no one* does this at a college fair, which is why you should. Most of the time you'll get some great advice; sometimes you may get a scholarship offer—but don't be surprised if they don't know what to say, since few students do this. Either way, you leave a strong impression. Leave them your contact information, tell them you hope they visit your high school soon, and move on.

Make quick notes about this college before you visit the next one; you don't want to have all the colleges blend together. This is easier to do at an online fair, but if you're at a face-to-face event, find a way to do this. It's crucial.

If you can get to seven to ten colleges and spend time at an information session, call it an evening with some post-fair pizza. You now have some solid information about which colleges are worthy of further investigation and some solid information on yourself as well—truly a dynamic duo.

CHAPTER 15

More Search Tools and One to Avoid

There are other great ways to scope out college possibilities without leaving home. Most of them are easy to access and most are very helpful, with just one to avoid. Read on.

A great way to find out more about a college is to let the college come to you. Many colleges send admissions representatives to high schools in the fall or spring to tell you about their college. These meetings can be in person, or they can be online. A list of these colleges is usually posted weekly somewhere in the counseling office, or online. Be sure to check the list every week, look up the colleges on their website or in a college guide (more on that soon), and then sign up to meet with the rep. In some high schools, reps are only allowed to meet with students at lunch, or before or after school, and some will only let reps meet with students in the lunchroom (which reps hate, but if they must, they must). If your school has these rules, give up your free time and go anyway. Not many students do this, which is (ready?) exactly why you should.

The same is true for hotel visits or online college visits held in the evening. Some reps have such tight schedules that they can only meet with lots of students in a local hotel ballroom in the evening or on the weekend. The same rules apply here: look up the school, see if it might work for you, and bring along your parents and pals for college information followed by ice cream.

No matter where you meet the rep, make sure you give them your contact information. Introduce yourself to the rep, and if it's any kind of high school visit, be prepared to be the only one in attendance. This happens more often that you think and can lead to a deep discussion and an interview with you the rep will long remember. Once the meeting is over, write down your impressions, and you're done.

We talked earlier about Big Future, and that's a great tool to use. It's a website where you can pick colleges based on all kinds of factors—location, major, cost, average grades, if they serve kosher food, the kind of sports teams they have—you name it.

If your school subscribes to SCOIR, you must do a college search on SCOIR. This search engine connects you with the social media sites of the college's clubs and organizations, so you don't just find out the college has a theater club and program—you get to interact with it. The career search tools on SCOIR also can't be beat.

Your counselor may have a college finder they like as well. These sites give you a good way to learn about colleges you don't know about, but this is just a starter tool. Follow up by visiting the college's website for sure.

College guides are another great source—books or magazines that describe what colleges have to offer. Guides usually give you a complete look at a college, including the classes, the social life, the town, what you need to be admitted, even interviews with students. Your high school and local library should have a ton of these, and there are some free ones to use online as well.

But while you're looking for the right guide, avoid the ones that rank colleges. There are some amazing colleges out there, to be sure, but deciding which one is "the best" is really something for you to figure out—and remember, the editors of the college guide have never met you.

Most of the rankings are based heavily on the opinions of college presidents, and what they have heard about other colleges. Now, college presidents are nice people, but it's likely they are familiar with fifty colleges tops—and they are totally unfamiliar with you. After about fifty or so, they're relying more on what others have told them about the college and less on direct information. That gets a little dicey.

You don't need to read a magazine to find out if Southwestern Michigan State is a great school; you need to read a magazine to help figure out if Southwest Michigan State is a great school for you. Guides help you do that, and rankings don't—so use the former, and skip the latter.

A Heads-Up on Chapters 16–18

Every student looking at colleges has their own list of what they're looking for. In some cases, those interests overlap the interests of others, and that's especially true if the student is thinking about being a college athlete, plans on studying the arts in college, or has learning differences they want to make sure the college can meet.

Chapters 16–18 provide some of the big ideas students need to think about if they're in one of these groups. It would be easy to write an entire book on all the special groups students identify with, but we're going to leave it at these three.

As you read the next three chapters, keep in mind that these aren't the *only* things students in these groups need to consider in their college choice. An art student isn't likely to be happy in college if they find the right professor but end up in a college that's too far from home for their liking. Similarly, an athlete may be thrilled to find a college where they can start varsity as a freshman, but that may not mean as much if there's nothing to do on campus over the weekend.

Too many college guides see athletes as only athletes, or think that students who need academic accommodations are defined solely by those needs. That's not the case, and the next few chapters are meant to give you some direction on what to think about in a college choice, without limiting who you are or what you choose.

CHAPTER 16

College Considerations for Fine and Performing Artists

The most popular college guides, fairs, and online search tools get many college seekers off to a good start, but leave them looking for more. A history major is looking for a college that specializes in Renaissance History; an anthropology major wants a good Forensics Anthropology program… and artists want something more than just a list of good art schools.

When it comes to help with niche majors, naval architecture majors get web links for majors of top schools and English horn majors get articles on why it's better to play the English horn than the oboe, but they don't get lists of colleges that could help them achieve these goals. Just ducky.

Serious high school artists are used to working a little harder to dig up the resources and opportunities they need to follow their interests, and college is no different. Artists, dancers, musicians, and metalsmiths alike would do well to connect these dots to find a college that will nurture the rhythm of their hearts:

Ask the right people. Most music, drama, dance, and art teachers have to get a degree in their specialty, and the truly committed arts teachers follow the current trends in college programs. Their insights into strong programs and your interests are a strong combination; the same is true if you take private lessons or study with someone outside of school. Polish this off with a trip to your counselor's office, and you're off to a good start. If they can't help you, their connections in the arts community should get you an answer faster than you can say presto.

Go to the right fairs. The National Association for College Admission Counseling (nacacnet.org) holds a series of visual and performing arts fairs each fall—in-person fairs if possible, online if not. College reps at these fairs have special insights into the artistic offerings at their colleges and can point you in the right direction.

Visual artists also have National Portfolio Days (nationalportfolioday. org), where you can take your work and get advice from art faculty and admissions officers on the work you've done to date, and where to go from there. These events can get a little crowded, but they're worth the wait.

Look at general colleges, too. Artists often focus on colleges or conservatories that only offer degrees in music, art, etc., but it's wise to look at colleges or universities that have strong arts programs as part of a larger choice of majors. Not only are there some great arts programs at general colleges, but they often also provide special talent-based scholarships some institutes can't afford. A general university is also something to consider if you know you want art to be some part of your life but not your entire living. You don't have to decide right now, but it's wise to keep your options open, and looking at general colleges does that.

Review audition and portfolio requirements. Admission requirements for arts programs vary, from heavy reliance on academic classes to "If you can draw, you're in." Since this mix differs widely from school to school—and since every school has different requirements for your audition or portfolio—make sure you know the expectations of each school. Portfolios are usually submitted as digital files of your work; ask your art teacher for the name of the top art/tech person who has the magic touch when it comes to putting your work in its best light.

CHAPTER 17

College Considerations for Athletes

Many students who want to play sports at college have been dreaming, thinking, and planning for their opportunity well before high school. At the same time, there are too may stories about athletes losing eligibility or opportunities to play, even when it's not their fault.

To make sure you get your field of dreams, follow these basics:

Know the rules. Most colleges belong to athletic associations with clear guidelines on eligibility, recruiting techniques, and visiting colleges. The best known set of guidelines is for the NCAA (ncaa.org). Check with the colleges you're interested in to see the set of guidelines they (and you) have to follow, and make sure you (and your parents) read those guidelines at least once a month, starting from the time you contact a college (or one contacts you) to the last day you play college ball.

Make sure you're academically eligible. Most colleges and athletic associations have minimum class, GPA, and test score requirements athletes have to meet in high school. Colleges will likely need transcripts and copies of test scores to make sure you qualify; others will have you register with the NCAA Clearinghouse to confirm your ability to play. Make sure you do your part early, and keep your grades up to the very end, since eligibility GPAs are calculated to the very end of senior year.

Be clear on how to contact a college. Colleges don't always reach out to athletes, so it's important to know when and how you should step up and introduce yourself to a coach and a program. Many contacts include a letter or email from you to the coach. Since many colleges are cutting back on recruiting travel, it's wise to send along a DVD or digital link of your work on the field, along with a résumé of your teams, championships, and awards. Videographers are out there who do this for a living, and your high school coach usually knows how to find them. Also, don't forget to ask your coach for help in finding a quality college or program. They often have the inside track to making introductions.

Going to campus? Plan ahead. Campus visits are a must for student athletes, provided the college allows you to come and it's safe to do so. In some cases, colleges will pay for you to visit. There are limits on when and how a college can do this, along with when and how they can be in touch with you. Make sure you don't fumble a choice by not knowing what you—and they—should or shouldn't be doing.

Get a clear understanding of their commitment. One student thought she was getting a guaranteed volleyball scholarship, when in fact she was one of fourteen freshmen competing for three spots on the team. She didn't make it, so her scholarship ended after one year. Since her family couldn't afford the tuition, she ended up going home.

Getting an offer to join a team—or better yet, a scholarship to play at college—is a real head rush, and a cause for celebration. After the initial thrill wears off, read the offer (which needs to be in writing) as closely as you read a financial aid offer (see chapter 51). If you don't know what the offer really says, ask the college. If what they say doesn't make sense, ask a coach, a counselor, or an attorney.

Get a clear understanding of your commitment. College athletes often have to meet with tutors and attend mandatory study halls, in addition to going to practices and classes that can take up five or six hours of every day. This level of discipline is often more than a student wants to give, since being a student athlete can sometimes seem more like a job than anything else. Once you know the college is willing to stand by its end of the agreement, make sure you're ready to stand by yours.

CHAPTER 18

College Considerations for Students with Special Needs

A successful college search for a student—any student—leads them to colleges that will offer the right mix of challenge and support. Also known as "fit," this is why water polo players who want to major in Chinese only apply to certain colleges. This is also true for students who may need extra time on tests, students who need an interpreter who knows sign language, or students who need to have a dorm room they can share with their service animal.

Everyone deserves a college that works for them. To make sure you're customizing your college search to include as many options as possible, follow these important steps:

Talk to your counselor early. All students should spend time talking college with their counselor, but if you have a special need, talk with your counselor early and often. The answers you need may best be found in their experience working with other students who have had a similar need, or in contacting other counselors. Give them the time they need to help you.

Ask the adults in your learning resource center. The aides and teachers helping you in high school have probably worked with other students who had special needs similar to yours. Use their wisdom to guide you in the right direction; they may even be able to connect you with former students who can give you the inside story on what to look for in a college.

Request ACT and SAT accommodations. Not every college requires these tests anymore, but it's still wise to take at least one of them. Both offer accommodations for students who apply for them, including extra time, extra breaks, readers, large-print editions, and more. You'll need to apply early, and you will likely have to supply some documentation for them to review your request. This may be done by your counselor or your high school's testing coordinator. Ask your counselor, and they will point you in the right direction.

Head for the web. A good first step is to simply do an online search for "Colleges for students with (ADHD, dyslexia, Asperger's). Like all searches, you need to be choosy. The best lists come from associations that offer a wide array of services (Asperger Foundation International, for example) or well-established college search sites. Keep looking at these lists until you see the names of a few colleges three or four times; that's the beginning of a strong list.

Hit the books. A number of guides are out there, in print and online, that will identify colleges that might be of interest, and many of these books offer insights on how to make a strong transition to college. A popular place to begin is the *K&W Guide to Colleges for Students with Learning Differences*. This guide tends to feature large public universities, but there's enough of a mix of schools for a good start. Combined with information on college websites, it can help you frame the questions you need to ask every college on your list.

Research, research, research. The kinds of services each college offers is best understood with a campus visit. Colleges may list what they offer on their website and in college guides, but students usually find great variation in the accommodations offered by different teachers and in different departments—and this is just as true for some colleges that have a strong reputation for being supportive of students with special needs. Visit if you can; if you can't, get on some video calls and talk with professors you'd likely work with in your major, and definitely talk with students who use the resources you are most likely to need.

You also need to know that, wherever you go, you'll need to advocate for yourself. The art and science of taking care of yourself is a life skill you should hone now. It's the best way to make sure you'll start, finish, and enjoy college.

CHAPTER 19

ACT and SAT

If there's any part of the college application that's changed dramatically, it's the role the SAT or ACT play in college admissions decisions. A generation ago, every college required one or the other, and only accepted one of the two tests. Then all colleges allowed you to submit scores from either one, but you still had to submit scores.

Then a real change started to happen. Many colleges looked at the information they were getting from test scores and decided they really didn't tell them all that much. Combined with all the stress students were going through to take a four-hour test—not to mention the cost of taking the test and sending the scores—many colleges decided to become test optional. Send the scores if you want to; if not, that's OK too.

A little over a thousand colleges were test optional before COVID hit, and then the number soared. Many colleges realized students couldn't take the test because test dates kept getting cancelled. Realizing that meant way fewer applicants, they went test optional for a year, or two, or three—or, in some cases, forever.

This means you really have to pay close attention to the testing requirements of every college you apply to. It isn't enough to assume their policy is the same as it was when your older sibling applied, or even last year; some have gone back to requiring tests, some haven't, and a few aren't looking at any test scores from anyone, even if you send them. Hit the website of every college you have in mind, and make sure you are looking at the testing requirements for the year you are applying. That's how much this is changing.

In general, the advice is for students to still take the tests, if they can do so safely. Since each test is a little different, you need to think about which one you should take. In a perfect world, you'd take each test once, figure out which one you did better on, and take that one a second time. That's a little too much money for some students; instead, they'll look at their PSAT scores, take an online practice ACT, and make a decision from there. That works, too.

Registration for both tests is online at collegeboard.com and actstudent.org. Most students take these tests in the spring of their junior year. There is a trend to take them once in December without much practice, and use those results to study for taking the test a second time in the spring of junior year. Both tests are also offered in the summer in case you want to focus on grades until school's out. But be careful— there tend to be fewer test centers in the summer, so it can be hard to find one in your area. Tests can also be taken senior year, but taking them in October means sending them in November, and that can be a little late when it comes to applying for college. Better to plan early and get them done well before senior year starts.

CHAPTER 20

Test Prep

Registering for the tests is easy; the harder part can be choosing how to prepare for them. There are a zillion options out there, so find the one that's right for you:

Timing. You want to consider when you're going to take the test. Both tests are designed to measure what students know at the end of junior year, so many students first take the test in March or April, discover which test they are more comfortable with, and take that one a second time in the summer. If that's the case, any test prep you may want to do should start no later than January. Keep in mind, I am a big fan of not doing any test prep and seeing how you score on the first test, but that assumes you're going to take one of the tests a second time.

A good number of students are now taking their first tests in December of junior year. This gives students time to get their scores back and use those scores to develop a test prep strategy for the second round of testing. If that's the case, and if you want to do some test prep before then, you'd likely want to think about starting in August. First semester of junior year is a pretty important semester, so the focus should be on grades. This isn't really a time to start test prep.

Retesting. Some people use the "take the test twice strategy" at a higher level, taking the test over and over and over again. Scores do tend to go up the second time, but after that, they don't really go up all that much unless you devote an incredible amount of time to studying just for the test. So seven times is out, unless there's a cutoff score for a scholarship.

Self-help. Between the free online websites, the test prep booklets, and the online sample tests, there are all kinds of ways to study at your own pace, but will you? It's easy enough to say you'll study on Saturday after your homework is done, but most students need some kind of parental assist with this ("You can have your cell phone back once you study").

Classes. Some classes teach you the content of the tests, other classes show you the "tricks" behind taking the test, and still others do both. Some run two days; others run fourteen weeks. Some are outrageously expensive; others are less outrageously expensive. If you go this route, ask for specific data—"You say your average student raises their test score four hundred points. What's the average for students who had PSAT scores like mine?" Also, ask about class scholarships or discounts for students from the same high school.

Tutors. Take your test scores to an experienced tutor, who can build a personalized plan focusing on the areas you need the most help with. You don't waste time with a class that overviews the entire test, and it can be cheaper than a full-blown class to boot.

Apply to a "test-optional" college. If testing isn't your thing, a test-optional college may be in your future. There are enough colleges out there that no longer require an ACT or SAT; the key is to make sure their test-optional policy will apply to you, since these policies often change from year to year. Get the latest information and make a strong decision. A great starter list of test optional colleges can be found at fairtest.org. Always check the college's website to confirm their test optional status.

The College Freak Factor is mighty high when it comes to test prep. Most students freak about the tests and do way too much prep, or they freak about giving up too much free time to study and do way too little. You have to do what's comfortable, and what you can afford in money and time, but this is the one area where students say, "If I had to do anything different, I would have studied more."

Just note they said study—not obsess.

CHAPTER 21

Senior Schedule and More on College Visits

By March of junior year, you've scheduled to take, or have taken, the ACT or SAT (if you're going to take them at all, and I still say that's a good idea), and you have at least three colleges you want to explore in depth. That leaves two other things to do: make your senior schedule and ask teachers to write you letters of recommendations (see chapter 31).

Your senior schedule has to do three things:

1. **Have all the classes you need to graduate from high school.** One key to getting into college is getting out of high school, so double-check your transcript, make sure you are literally good to go, and count your gym credits twice—they're slippery.

2. **Keep you challenged during all of senior year.** Speaking of gym, remember what coach always says: play to the whistle. If you take a soft schedule, you'll forget about thinking, studying, writing, and organizing your time. You'll then spend the first semester of college trying to ramp up these skills, along with

learning how to do laundry, getting yourself out of bed, and calling your parents often enough that they'll remember you at Thanksgiving. A bad start in college is like a bad start in ninth grade—it's tough to catch up. You're in shape, so stay in shape, and just say no to schedule sludge. If you've run out of tough classes to take in high school, take some at a local college. In some states, your high school will even pay for the courses.

3. **Show the colleges you're serious about learning.** The folks who take a "checklist" approach to college take three hard years of courses in high school, and maybe in the first semester of senior year, but then out come six sections of History of Pizza. The college of your dreams will see this epidemic on your final transcript—yes, they will see one—and if your final grades go down a lot (say, A- average to B-) or if your schedule is soft, they'll think you've changed your mind about learning, so they might change their mind about you. Try it if you dare; it happens.

With the goals of junior year taken care of, let's talk a little more about visiting campuses. Some students have dreams about going to faraway campuses—you wouldn't believe how many juniors in Michigan talk about the University of Hawaii—but they can't get there to visit. In addition, many families can't afford to visit faraway campuses, even if they aren't across the ocean. They can visit the local ones, but the distant ones are a bit of a stretch.

Thanks to the power of online tours, you don't have to worry about this as much as students before you. Still, if it's safe to travel, and you really want to see the place for yourself, it's time to put Plans B and C into place. Plan B is simple: wait until April of senior year to visit colleges. By then, you'll know most of the colleges you've been admitted to, so the number you need to visit will be smaller. Since this eliminates the number of colleges you'll be able to see as a junior, this plan isn't perfect, but there may be enough local colleges to give you a taste for the kinds of colleges that are out there, and that helps.

Plan C is even simpler: let someone else pay for it. If one of your (healthy) pals is heading out by car to tour a campus, offer to split the cost of gas and go with them. If you're worried their opinion about the college might bias you, talk about that before you go. A true friend will understand, and you'll be able to work something out.

If you're the first in your family to go to college, or if you're a member of an underrepresented group of students on campus, the college might be willing to pay for your visit. Fly-in programs are a big deal at even some of the smallest colleges, and all you have to do is fill out a form to ask. Now that's a bargain.

CHAPTER 22

Making the List

It's now spring of junior year or, better yet, summer(!), so it's time to put on your favorite sweats or workout shorts, grab a box of cereal, put on a little Miles Davis (seriously, if you leave college without an appreciation for jazz, it's been a waste of your time), and crash on the couch.

At this stage, you're heading into the home stretch of the first part of the college search. By studying hard, giving back, thinking about your place in the world, and having fun, your high school years have been great to experience and great to grow on—something to build not just a college application on but also for applying yourself once you're in college, and once you're out. Because you built these qualities up over time, you're not burned out about college; because your parents and your counselor are on board with you, they're not on your case; and because you've learned about the colleges in great detail, you're focused on finding schools that are right for you, not finding ones that are "right" colleges.

You really need to hold on tightly to that last thought from now until June of your senior year. Lots of well-meaning folks at the family reunion, neighborhood barbecue, or Custard Cone will ask you where you're going to go and what you're going to major in. If you don't give them the answer they want to hear—that you'll be majoring in business at one of "those" colleges—they will likely do things with their faces you swore were limited to cartoon characters who eat too many Cocoa Doodles for breakfast.

Of course, it's fine to major in business at a name college—if that's right for you—but if that's not where you are, that's not where you should go. Don't get me wrong; the last thing you want to do is go to college without thinking about your plans. But if you've thought about them and don't have a major, finding a college that doesn't care if you have one right now *is* a plan—even if it's at a college people haven't heard of, and even if you change your major a lot once you're there (which most students do, even the business majors).

Keeping your focus in the midst of all these opinions, mosquitoes, and charred burgers may not be the easiest thing to do, so you need to focus on something else. As you start your transition summer and continue to research colleges, remember your goal is to come to high school the first day of senior year with two things:

1. A killer tan
2. A list of four to eight colleges you'd like to apply to, which includes
   a. at least one college in your home state;
   b. two colleges where your grades (and if it applies, test scores) are above the averages for most of the students admitted there;
   c. a couple of dream schools you can't quite figure out how you'll get into or pay for;
   d. all colleges you'll be happy to go to.

We'll talk about the list over the next few chapters, as well as some college options you likely haven't considered. For now, dream on, keep thinking, be strong in the work you have done so far…and don't forget to fish out the cereal that landed in the cracks between the sofa cushions.

Also write your list down, and put it somewhere you can see it every day.

CHAPTER 23

Likely Schools and Transferring

Most students don't beef too much about applying to an in-state college. If you've researched or visited any local colleges, you've likely found one or two that will work for you if you choose to stay close to home, either to be close to family or because in-state colleges are an amazing bargain. You might have the heart of a Banana Slug, but hearts are a funny thing, and by April, being a Sooner or a Spartan or a Hustlin' Quaker may be just as wonderful, even if home is just an hour away—or because home is just an hour away.

The real hustle I get with students is when I advise them to apply to two likely schools—places where, based on grades and maybe test scores, you're in the middle of the pack of all applicants, if not a little ahead of them. Students find nice ways to express this, but it basically boils down to this:

"Why would I want to go to a school where I'm the smartest student?"

I get it. Good students want challenge, and they think the best way to get that challenge is to go to school with students who are smarter than they are. Other students worry about "likely" schools because they think no one will hire them or admit them to med school if they have a degree from a college no one has heard of.

So why likely schools? First, finding a college you like and know you can get into (and a likely school has to be both) gives you confidence to apply to other colleges—it's the rock you build on while completing your other applications. September might tell you it's cool just to apply to tough schools, but February and March seem a lot colder than usual if every application that could be a yes could just as easily (or more likely) be a no. Likely schools school you on how applications work and give you the "Yes!" factor you need to take on applications that have eighty-six parts.

Second, dough and prestige. Lots of competitive colleges offer automatic scholarships to students with high grades and, in some cases, high test scores. Right-- you automatically get some college cash, no matter who you are, or if you financially need it. In addition, a student who's stronger than most can find their way into a good college's honors college or advanced scholars courses. These mean smaller classes, better profs, and fellow students who are going to challenge you just the way you need challenging. Looking for an opportunity where you can be given a run for your money? This is it.

Finally, there's the two-college strategy. Highly selective colleges are crazy competitive. The main reason students don't get admitted is because the college runs out of room before they run out of great students. Since very small differences make the difference at these schools, students choose a different plan: start at a likely school and then transfer to their dream school.

You have to be careful here. Most highly competitive colleges are even harder to get into as a transfer student, and you have to watch the classes you take at School #1, since not all classes transfer to another college. This also means you have to go through the application process twice, and transfer deadlines differ for transfer students.

Still, this is a growing trend—start local, stoke the GPA, save some dough, and off you go. If you transfer enough credits from College #1, your transfer college may not even look at your high school transcript, so this is also a way to get a fresh start. Either way, watch your classes, get good grades, and remember the transfer option.

CHAPTER 24

Is College Worth It?

It's July, and you may be done with school, but it doesn't seem like school is done with you. ACT scores are back, your parents want you to start your college essays, and your late summer job plans have just fallen through. You open your email, and you've received your schedule for next year: five academic classes, one honors class, and two Advanced Placement (AP) classes. If all goes well, you'll be admitted to a college that's right for you, where you'll get to do this for four more years.

"Dude," you say to yourself, "is college worth it?"

Your parents come back from a dinner party in the neighborhood. "I ran into Jenny Smithers," your mom says. "She graduated from State U this spring with honors in architecture, but with the slow job market, she's having a tough time finding a job, and living at home."

"She's the eighth college grad in the neighborhood who came back home," says Dad. "One more and the unemployed college grads can start a baseball team."

"Dude," you say to yourself, "is college worth it?"

You take a break from job hunting to catch the end of the golf match on TV. As you're flipping the channels, you stop at a story that talks about Bill Gates, Abe Lincoln, and some woman in Connecticut. The story says Bill Gates didn't finish college and Abe Lincoln never started, but this woman in Connecticut took out $115,000 in loans to go to college. She now has a bachelor's degree in philosophy and can't get a job.

"Dude," you say to yourself.

You head back to the computer and make a scientific investigation. It turns out that the unemployment rate is lowest for students with college degrees. It also turns out that most of the job growth in the next ten years will come in jobs requiring training after high school, but not a four-year degree. It also turns out the average graduate with a bachelor's degree has $30,000 in college loans.

"Whoa!" says you.

You've decided your homework can wait, and you head down to Maggie's Pizza. Dave's the manager on duty tonight, and he's the smartest guy you know.

"'Sup, bro?" he says, without looking up from the pizza he's cutting.

"Dave, is college worth it?"

Dave looks up, puts down the pizza cutter, and wipes his hands on his apron.

"Let's see. Moved in the day before classes started, and I was so scared, I didn't unpack till November twelfth. My roommate was from Brooklyn, and he taught me how to eat pizza the right way. Read my first book of poetry. Worked my summers cleaning dorm rooms, and swore I'd never do that again. Went to Scotland for three weeks and got to see the sun set at midnight. Learned how to footnote a paper, why camels spit, how to write the business plan that led to this store and the four others in the chain, and why it matters to me who wins the elections in Turkey."

"What happened November twelfth?"

"I met Maggie."

"Hmm."

"What about you, man? You know what you want to study?"

"No."

"Where you want to live?"

"No."

"Do for a living?"

"No."

"Yeah. That's about where I was before I went. Slice to go?"

Dave shows you how to eat pizza Brooklyn style, and you head for home.

"Where've you been, champ? You need to find a job."

"Sorry, Dad. Just needed to clear my head."

"Well, it's a busy time for you."

"Yeah. Hey, Dad?"

"Yes?"

"Who's running for president in Turkey?"

CHAPTER 25

Have You Cleaned Up Your Social Media Pages Yet?

There are three technology rules when it comes to applying to college:

1. Use an online application. It's faster, you make fewer mistakes, and online help is there when you need it.
2. Create a new email account just for college applications and college communications. This keeps all your college information—and only your college information—in one place, and once you're done applying, your regular email isn't choked with posts you don't need.
3. Clean up any and all social media pages you have, and keep an eye on what others are posting about you.

Students understand the first two with no problem. College applications need to be clean, clear, and thorough, so it's important to make sure you're sending colleges your application essays, not your prom pictures.

Ditto for the new email account. This may seem a little old school to you, but email is still the way most colleges communicate with students—so that's where you need to be. This makes it easy to keep track of your college information, and it's probably best the college doesn't know your personal email address is *ladiesgoforme@mymail.com*.

Students usually get a little confused when we talk social media accounts. They insist colleges don't care about your media presence and are too busy to look at a student's accounts. To prove it, they will ask the colleges if they look at online accounts, and the colleges will say no.

Fair enough, except when I asked a college rep if they looked at a student's online presence, they said, "Do you really think I'd tell you if we did?" Keep in mind that, for a number of reasons, admissions offices that don't review online accounts end up looking at you online anyway if, for some reason, they find out about a post you've made that is making the rounds. Like the swimmer who came home from a bad practice and wrote on social media on how awful his coach was. The student lost his scholarship the next day.

Play it safe. Rough language, risky pictures—even an account under another name—can hurt you and anyone else who's in questionable photos with you. Once you've tidied up yours, ask your friends who have anything iffy about you on their pages to clean things up as well. After that, search for yourself on the web and see what's there. You might not need to address it, or even do anything about it, but it's better to know what's there before the colleges do.

And don't forget, social media can be an agent of good when you're applying to college. Artists can create online galleries with pictures, art, or poetry; athletes can create an online brag book; scientists can discuss their research. This is as easy as adding the web address to your application.

Either way, be careful with this; you never know…

(Based on a true story)

Joanna thought she was all that.
She knew she was a winner;
A 3.9 for a GPA,
That girl was no beginner!
Took five APs and tutored too,
Her homework was a snap;
Spent most nights on the internet
Just dishing out some smack.
She posted pix of homecoming
Her folks would see as knockouts,
But, hey, they'd never see them since
Her online page was blocked out.

You can't imagine her surprise
When her counselor said, "Hey, lady,
I got a call from East Coast U;
This news will make you crazy!
The U was going to let you in
When in arrived their intern.
'This girl's all over the internet
With pix to make your eyes burn.'
The intern loaded up a page
Of some homecoming hijinks,
And in the photos, there was you—
They made our rep do eye blinks!

"They saw your pictures once or twice
And thought they'd overlook it,

But then they read your online smack
And that's what really cooked it.
Your essays were all erudite
And very nicely tailored,
But when they saw the real you
Has language like a sailor.
They read your app and loved you, girl;
It's you they were admittin',
But now they say they just can't take
A profane party kitten."

So students, listen—hear me out!
Few colleges go lookin',
But if bad web vibes come their way
That just can't be mistooken,
Your full-ride dough, your dream admit
Are going down to zero
And all because you had to be
A bad-selfed online hero.

CHAPTER 26

Community Colleges and Grade Point Averages

Another group of colleges to consider for your list are community colleges...and once again, I guess it's your turn to speak.

"Junior colleges? Isn't that where they teach, like, dog grooming and motorcycle safety?"

First of all, they aren't called junior colleges anymore (if you're looking for someone to say using that name was a bad idea, my hand is clearly raised). Second, community colleges exist to serve the learning needs of the community, meeting a huge need in this country. While a lot of media attention is focused on the eight colleges of the Ivy League, far more—far, *far* more—students attend community colleges, and you should be very glad they do.

Community colleges are based on this wacky notion that learning doesn't stop at age twenty-two. Time goes by, and people change. You thought high school was dull, and you took a job that made great money. But now the magic of the money has faded, and you've found something else you want to do. Community college meets your needs.

You want to go to a four-year college out of state, but something—family needs, the need to work, the cost of tuition—requires you to stay home for a year or two first. Community college meets your needs.

You've heard that a one- or two-year certificate can land you a job that pays more than most four-year college grads, and you'll finish your schooling with much less debt. Community college meets your needs.

If you decide to start at a community college with the goal of transferring to another college, keep a very close eye on your classes. The courses you might need to get a community college degree might not transfer to your next school—and if they do, they may just transfer as electives and not for specific credit.

This is why you need to work closely with your *next* college as well. Get a copy of their transfer guide, which often lists the specific courses you need to take at community college to stay on track for a four-year degree. These courses can change quickly, so be sure to touch base with your next college once a semester.

And if the community college says you need to take a course or two before you can take transferrable courses, do it. The only reason they're suggesting you do this is to make sure you can pass the transferrable courses—and the last thing you want your next college to see is a string of low grades.

With that taken care of, just a word or two about your high school GPA. It's pretty safe to say most high schools have their own unique approach to calculating GPAs. Some add points for honors classes, others don't; some add points for a "plus" (as in B+), others don't. Some changed all their grades to pass/fail during the COVID crisis and never changed them back, others didn't.

If you think this makes the colleges crazy, you're right. How exactly can they figure out if you've taken challenging classes and how you really did in them?

This is why colleges ask for your high school's profile, a one-page introduction to your high school that includes the grading scale it uses, and describes the most challenging classes your high school offers. Ask for a copy of this the next time you're in your high school counseling office. It will help you know what the college understands about you and your high school.

This is also why many, many colleges recompute your GPA, using their own scale. Like high schools, some colleges give more points for an honors class, while others don't. Either way, it's important to ask just how each college does this. If they tell you they're looking for a 3.5 for most students, that's based on the way they calculate your GPA, not your high school. That could be a huge difference, so ask.

CHAPTER 27

Application Deadlines

In addition to building a college list based on GPA, cost, location, major—you name it—you might want to think about when the application is due and when you hear back from the college. Applying to schools that only give you a decision in April might seem OK at first, but most students who get to Christmas without a college admission tend to freak out a little.

Here's the menu of options to consider:

First come, first served (Rolling Admissions). The sooner your complete application is submitted at a rolling admissions institution, the sooner they review it and send you a decision. In many cases, this means applying in September gives you an answer by October. Be careful here—rolling admissions schools can be harder to get into the longer you wait. So if a rolling college has a February 1 deadline, applying in September is still a good idea.

First come, first served, sort of (Early Action, or EA). EA gives you an early deadline—typically around November 1—to apply. All applications submitted by then are read together, and decisions go out together, sometimes in December but more often in January. With EA, you get a decision earlier, but you still have a lot of time—typically until May 1—to pick which college is right for you.

First committed, first served (Early Decision, or ED). ED is like EA, but with one *big* difference. Like EA, you apply early and hear back early. However, if you apply ED and are accepted, *you must attend that college.* Once an ED college says yes and meets your demonstrated financial need (as defined by them, not you), you have to withdraw your applications to all your other colleges, and your college search is over. Welcome home!

First come and first committed, first served (typically known as Single Choice Early Action). Single choice is like EA, except this becomes the one and only college you can apply to early—no other EA schools, no ED schools. Some colleges have different rules for single choice that allow for a little wiggle room, so read their website carefully about deadlines. If admitted to a single choice school, you still have time (May 1) to decide, but this does limit your early applications.

Y'all come, y'all served (Regular Admission). These colleges establish a common deadline (usually around January 1), and all applications are read at the same time. Decisions usually come out until April 1st, and you have until May 1st or so to choose.

Since some colleges have more than one deadline, you want to study your options carefully and make sure you apply to the deadline right for you. Early programs give you the advantage of showing a college you're really interested in them, but ED requires an early commitment that you might not want to take on.

It's also true that many colleges take a larger percentage of their students through early programs, since that helps them plan for the coming school year. Since a smaller number of students apply to early programs, a college that takes a third or more of their class early means they're taking a bigger number of students from a smaller application pool. That's usually an incentive to apply early action, for sure.

You'll want to find out if any of your colleges defer any students who apply early. We'll talk more about deferral later; basically, it means they want more information about your application before they make a decision. Some colleges will defer some early applicants, but others will just offer a yes or no. It's important to ask about that as you build your list.

So, do you apply early? Figuring this out from a "what are my chances" point of view can be tricky since every year is different, and many colleges change the percentage of early students they take from year to year. As a rule of thumb, apply EA if you love a school, and apply ED if you want to marry the school. After that, try to see the percentage of students the college took early last year. If it's above one third, you may want to consider applying early, even if the college isn't among your top choices. This will keep your options open, and that's what this is all about.

No matter what you choose, remember that deadlines are real. An application with a January 1 deadline won't get read if it's submitted January 2, so plan ahead.

CHAPTER 28

College Costs

Now that you're working on your final list, you (or your parents) are probably thinking about how you're going to pay for college. This is bad, bad, good, and bad:

It's bad if you decide not to scope out a school just because you think you can't afford it. Many colleges have ways of making a pricey place affordable, but you won't know that without talking to someone in their financial aid office, or looking online. In addition, you explore a college to see if it's right for you, and along the way, you learn more about yourself. If researching Megabucks College leads you to realize you're interested in archaeology, you can use that information to explore colleges with great archaeology programs that are more affordable. If you don't explore Megabucks U, you don't learn about an important part of yourself.

It's also bad to pass on the high end, because the high end might be cheaper. A parent called to scold me for encouraging her child to apply to a college they couldn't afford, and she wanted me to "recommend" a cheaper college instead. The pricey school was perfect for the student, and she applied, hoping to get one of the college's full scholarships. There were only ten available, but that didn't matter because she only needed one—and got it. That made college free.

At the same time, it's also good to build your list with money in mind. The student did indeed apply to that lesser-priced college and would have been incredibly happy there if the scholarship hadn't come through at the other college. A few big-cost colleges on your list is fine; all big-cost colleges on your list suggests you might be looking at name and prestige more than the things that really matter like major, fit, and reality. Dream? You bet, but a dream is only one kind of vision, and you need all kinds of views when putting together a strong college list.

Finally, it's also bad if now is the first time your parents are considering how to pay for college. Like most big expenses, planning ahead is good, even though it may seem easier to just hope something will work out because, sometimes, it doesn't. If your family has a financial planner, it's long past time for a visit. If they don't, a call to the financial aid office of one of your schools can be just as helpful.

You're going to want to spend at least part of a twenty-minute meeting looking at an online scholarship search site, such as finaid.org. Each of these sites provides an overview of how to apply for financial aid, from filing the Free Application for Federal Student Aid (FAFSA) to see if you qualify for federal financial aid, to applying through your college to see if they can help pay for it. You can also search for scholarships on these sites, and they often have articles on what not to do when applying for financial aid.

Every college also has a net price calculator (NPC) that allows you to put in a few figures (your income, etc.) and gives you an estimate of how much you would have to pay to go to that college. Keep in mind these are estimates, and many NPCs don't include scholarships you might earn because of high grades or because you have a special talent. So NPCs give good hints, but not all the answers.

Finally, remember that you can turn down part of a financial aid offer from a college, and accept the rest. If the loan part of a package seems too big, for example, you can say no to that part, and take the other parts. It's now up to you to figure out how to pay for the part the loan covered, but turning part of an aid package down is always an option.

It's true that money is a tool with power, but so is a chainsaw, and that isn't getting in the way of finding a great school. Like all power tools, treat it with respect, and you'll do fine.

CHAPTER 29

More on the Twenty-Minute Meeting about College Costs

So you've discovered net price calculators and their limits. That's a great start to understanding college costs. Here are some other key points to focus on when talking with your parents about paying for college:

Know your EFC. Nearly every college will require you to apply for federal financial aid before they even think about giving you any of their money, which means you'll have to fill out the FAFSA. It's free, and when you're done, they will give you a very important number— the expected family contribution, or EFC. This is what the federal government thinks you can afford to pay for college, no matter where you go. It's also the number many—that's many—colleges will use in deciding how much aid they can give you. So, if your EFC is $15,000, and State U is $20,000, you pay $15,000, and State U puts together a package to pay for the rest. If East Coast U costs around $45,000, you still pay $15,000. If community college costs $3,000, you pay for all of it. You can get a pretty good idea what this number will be by putting some key figures into the Fafsa4Caster on the web.

Be careful with this number. If you think it may make expensive colleges more affordable, you're right—it may. Since East Coast College has to find more money for you, there's a good chance their package might include more loan, or more money you earn by taking a job on campus (work study). Just how much loan and work study you get is up to each college, and you'll have to pay off or work off those parts of the package. Compare with care.

Think total price. There's more to going to college than paying for tuition, so make sure you know what the full *cost of attendance* will be. This consists of tuition, room and board, books, fees, and travel. Many scholarships are tuition only; others cover all costs and are known as full-ride scholarships. Make sure you know the total price for all your colleges.

More college data. It can help to know just how much help a college can give you. This could include knowing the average financial aid package, if the college offers loan-free financial aid (many do), what the average loan is in the packages they offer, and if they meet full need. This last question is important. Going back to East Coast U, if you need $30,000 from them, and they don't meet all need, they may only offer you $25,000 and hope you'll find a way to pay for the gap of $5,000. Families typically meet this gap by taking out even more loans, so watch out. Too many loans can weigh down your plans for life after college; it also can just plain weigh you down.

Merit scholarships. Parents often want to know if a college offers scholarships to kids for just being smart. Known as merit scholarships, many colleges do indeed offer these—and while it's not the reason you should go to a college, it's good to know they're out there. A nice list of these schools can be found at scholarships.com and cappex.com, although both require you to create a free account to find out about these opportunities.

Things change every year, so apply every year. College policies and programs on financial aid are always shifting, and your finances do the same thing. This is one of the reasons why you apply for financial aid every year, even if you're already getting it. Many colleges will actually offer you more money the longer you're in college, since you're now more likely to graduate, and they really want to see that happen.

The good news is that most of the forms you fill out only have to be updated—they'll have your old information on them, so you make the changes, and you're done. Considering you get a college education in return, that sounds like a bargain.

CHAPTER 30

The Twenty-Minute Meeting After That (College Costs, Part Three)

Now that you've found a way to talk with your parents about college costs, there's a good chance this will become a regular part of your college meetings—and if you think they were sweating a lot when they told you where babies come from, just wait.

It's hard for parents to talk to their children about money for college. Heck, it's hard for adults to talk about money with anyone. College is a particularly tough issue because most families don't save enough for college, so when it comes time to pay up, they're often a little short—sometimes more than a little short. Since parents can see college is coming up sooner or later (it's not like the dishwasher breaking out of the blue), that can lead to some serious parental guilt. I'm a bad parent for not saving enough; I don't make enough money; I'm a failure in life.

Help your parents by focusing on the subject at hand. "OK, so the financial aid estimator says we can afford this much. With the savings we all have and the money we all make at work, can we realistically make this happen?" Note that the conversation is about "we," the first sign your parents get that shows they aren't doing this alone. That's more important than you think—not only does it let them know you're invested (literally) into going to college; it also makes you focus and realize that going to college can have some long-term effects on your financial future.

It's also important to remember that paying for college is all about what you know and what you don't know. Colleges will offer financial aid packages with different amounts of grant (don't pay back) and loan (pay back)—packages you haven't seen yet. You may or may not go on to graduate school, so you want the loan part to be small, unless you're going into a field where the starting salaries will allow you to pay back those loans in a short amount of time. But you don't know what you want to major in, and your parents are hoping to retire some day and eat more than mac and cheese at every meal.

A key to dealing with the unknown is time. Your parents may need a week off after this meeting just to take a breath, seek out some help (like a financial planner), and get some answers. Doing some online research on merit scholarships might help, so consider doing that for twenty minutes during the week.

At some point, you're going to talk more about money for college, probably once you get all your financial aid offers. Compare these packages closely, and if you don't understand them, call the financial aid office. These are very thoughtful people, not robots, and they want you to come to their college. If explaining your financial aid offer three times will help you do that, that's what they will gladly do.

Once you're in college, continue the search for college cash by looking for unadvertised opportunities. Students can become lab assistants or dorm advisers after freshman year, and these jobs can include free room and board. Other off-campus jobs may open up as well, depending on who you talk to and how the economy is going.

Keep looking and listening…and don't give up right now on a college just because it seems out of reach.

It takes more than one person to make a dream come true, and your parents are already on board. Build your list with two affordable colleges—colleges you can pay for by yourself or colleges you can pay for with the least amount of help—and let the other colleges help you as much as they can. You're doing your part; let them do theirs.

CHAPTER 31

Letters of Recommendation— Nuts and Bolts

Now that your list is complete, it's time to get busy. Not every college requires letters of recommendation—in fact, there are more that don't want letters than do. At the same time, having one on hand is a good idea for a couple of reasons:

- It could help you get admitted. Colleges that don't ask for letters usually don't mind if you send one. If you're applying to a school where your grades (and maybe test scores) make you a "maybe," extra words of support from a teacher who knows you well are right there for the admissions committee to consider— and those could push you over the top.
- You may change your mind soon. Suppose you stop by a college on your way home from Aunt Marge's over Thanksgiving weekend and you love this place, but it requires letters of recommendation and has a December 1st deadline. If you plan

ahead for the possible, your letters are waiting for you, and your new dream stays alive.

- You may change your mind later on. If you transfer or put college off for a while, your college may still want recommendations from high school. If you ask teachers to write those letters now, they'll write about you based on fresh memories, not on how (or if) they remember you two years from now—and for as much as they like you, time can make a difference.

- You may need it for money. Once you're through applying for college, you'll probably be filling out forms for scholarships. Many scholarship applications require letters of recommendation, and having one that's ready to go can make all the difference in finding cash for college.

Some students freak out about asking for letters, but it's pretty easy. Check your colleges to see if they have any specific requirements about letters. Colleges that want letters generally ask for two, and they almost always want them from teachers of academic subjects who taught you in junior or senior year. Some engineering programs will want to hear from a math or science teacher. Otherwise, any academic subject is fine; if two letters are required, it's best not to send two from the same academic subject.

Unless your school has a different policy, you should ask for these in the spring of the junior year by talking to your teacher privately and in person (or online if school is just online) and asking them if they can write you a good letter of recommendation. The word "good" is important here. Any teacher can write you a letter, but if it's just going to be a list of your accomplishments and grades, that won't help. You want a letter from someone who knows you as a person and as a student—that makes a good letter. If a teacher honestly feels they can't write you a good letter, they'll tell you that in a gentle way. Don't be crushed; they're really helping you since weak letters of recommendation are usually worse than no letter at all.

If you've really been making the most of high school, if you've really been learning and living instead of just getting good grades, you're sure to have at least two or three relationships with teachers that are more than papers and grades. You won't feel close to all your teachers (and vice versa), but if spring of junior year rolls around and you have no teachers who know at least a little bit about your soul, that's bad—not because it looks bad to the colleges, but because you've had three years to learn about the world through the eyes and experiences of some pretty thoughtful, caring people. That kind of wisdom is too good to pass up.

CHAPTER 32

Letters—Nuts and Bolts

As you think about who you should ask to write your letters, you need to keep a couple of things in mind. As mentioned last chapter, most colleges will let you choose which academic teachers to ask, but some colleges will require a letter from an English teacher, and some technical schools will want to hear from a math or science instructor. All your letters should be from teachers in academic subjects; if you're applying as an arts student, a letter from your art instructor would likely be a great additional letter. If in doubt, ask the college. It's also good for all students to have a letter from someone who can talk about your writing.

If the college asks for two letters, it's really best to send just two. Additional letters tend to repeat what the first two letters have to say, and that drives colleges crazy. If you are convinced you have to include a third letter, check the college's website to see if that's OK. If it doesn't say anything, call and ask the college—and if that idea bothers you, that suggests maybe you don't need a third letter after all.

Once your letter writer gives you the OK, thank them, and let them know when you need the letter. In some cases, you'll have a September deadline for letters, and a good letter takes about three weeks to prepare. By giving your letter writers plenty of time to prepare, you are giving them the respect they are due, and you are helping them help you. That's why it's best to ask in the spring of your junior year.

If the colleges have forms that the letter writers must also complete, make sure you give them that form or send them the link to the online form. Give these to your letter writers at least three weeks before they're due. It's OK for them to send the same letter to different colleges, but each college may have a different form. If the letters can't be sent online (this doesn't happen very often), you need to give your letter writers envelopes addressed to the college, complete with two stamps. This way the writer completes the form, inserts the letter, and puts it in the mail.

Easy...and this way, you don't see the letters, which is good because you're not supposed to. In asking for a letter of recommendation, you're asking a teacher to write a letter about you, not to you. If this is a shock to you, remember that this is how letters work in the real world. You'll soon fill out job applications where employers will want to talk to friends and former bosses without you knowing what they'll say.

At some point, colleges will ask you if you want to see the letters of recommendation once you're admitted. In the United States, you won't get to see them now for any reason, but in some cases, you might get to see them once you're enrolled at that college. You want to *waive* that right. Teachers tend to write stronger letters when they know students will never see them, and some colleges will become suspicious if a student doesn't waive their right. Why would a student ask for a letter from a teacher they don't trust? Since the only time you could see the letter is once you're admitted, it's best to waive the right and move on.

Be sure to write a thank-you note (or email, I suppose) to your letter writers once your application is complete. Be sure to follow up with them once you hear back from the colleges, whether you're admitted or not. You asked them to write a letter for you because they care about you, so they'll be curious to know how things turned out.

CHAPTER 33

Online Errors to Avoid and Using One Application for Many Colleges

Just about all college applications are now online, something that doesn't surprise most students who have been texting all their lives. You'll likely have no problem completing the information, but there are a couple of crucial spots where students get hung up—so don't let these derail your plans:

"Save" versus "Submit." Nearly all online apps let you work on them a little at a time, save that part, and come back to the app later on. That way, you don't have to complete the application in one sitting—but here's the thing. Once you're done and ready to send the application, it's likely you will once again hit Save, when what you really want to do is hit Submit. Save keeps the application in a holding file; only Submit will get it in the hands of the admissions office. Once you're good to go, hit Submit, and look for an email from the college in one or two days confirming they have it. If you don't hear from them by then, first check to make sure you hit Submit (it happens), and then call to see if they have it.

Making payment. Many parents aren't crazy about paying for things online. Colleges respect that, so most will also give you a way to pay for your application with a phone call or through the mail—just make sure you do it. Mom, Dad, or you may get so caught up in the hoopla of applying to college, you'll forget to send in the payment—and without the dough, your app won't go. Pay after you apply.

Some colleges let students use a website where you can apply to more than one college. The best known of these applications is the Common Application.

These sites are great for students applying to several colleges—after all, how many times do you really want to fill out your name and address? Still, there are four things to keep in mind when using these platforms:

Each application may have its own additional essays. Sites like these may let you submit a basic essay to every college, but some colleges will want more writing samples than just one. Since these supplemental essays can add up in a hurry, make sure you know how much writing you really need to do for each college.

Each application has its own payment. You may be filling out one application, but each college has its own policy about application fees. Some will be free, but others won't be. Make sure you know what you owe and to which colleges.

Get everyone's email right. Multicollege sites often ask for the names and emails of your counselor and letter writers—this way, they only have to fill out one form, too! This works well, as long as they have the right email; if not, your counselor and teachers never get their forms and never write their letters. Double-check their emails, and type them in slowly.

Be sure to waive your rights. We touched on this before, but it's really important to check the "I waive my rights to see these letters" box on a multicollege app because once you check it, you can't change it—and that answer is submitted *before* you submit the application. If you answer incorrectly and change your mind later on, you'll have to send a letter—by US mail—to every college indicating you changed your mind, and that can really slow things up.

CHAPTER 34

The Biggest Hurdle Is the First Application

If you completed the college application mentioned in the Introduction, you know that filling out an application is actually pretty easy. Unfortunately, most students hit the application wall when a counselor isn't around, usually on a Saturday morning as they bring a laptop to the breakfast table, pour yet another bowl of Cocoa Doodles, decide it's time to apply to college, and freeze when they get to "Name."

In other words, they are overwhelmed by the "college is crazy" hype and are convinced this is just too hard.

I'm sorry I can't be at the breakfast table when there's nowhere to run to, but if I were there, I'd tell you to go to your room.

Truth is, most students balk at filling out a college application because it's the first time they realize that going to college, at least for them, means they will be leaving home. That's easy to understand. This is the place where you listen to your music, text your friends long after your parents have gone to bed, and think about your life. The world outside has changed and challenged you, sometimes in ways you didn't like or didn't completely master, but you always had home to sort out what it all really meant and looked forward to what came next. Giving this place up won't be easy.

The good news is that the colleges that are right for you will feel like home. It may be in the residence halls, it may be in the library (hey, it happens), it may be anywhere and everywhere on campus, but somewhere at those colleges, there is a spot waiting for you to reflect on the challenges of life, consider the possible, and text your pals until dawn. Once you think about college as your next home, the applications will be as easy as taking the written exam for your driver's license. Both are just the paperwork that leads to a greater sense of freedom. Going to college isn't about leaving home. It's about taking home with you.

The second thing I would do is replace your earbuds with sound-proof headphones. The application to a college the student loves often ends up in the shredder when a neighbor asks, "Where is that college?" or Uncle Bob reports that college is nowhere to be found in recently published college rankings. If it turns out no other student in your high school is applying to this place, the trifecta for trauma is complete.

When this happens, I encourage students to do the mature thing, and be selfish. By fall most college-bound seniors have a good sense of who they are and what they want next in life. Knowing what you know about yourself and your college choice, it's important to keep the well-meaning comments of others in perspective. Some may know you, some may know colleges, but very few (parents excepted) will know both as well as you do, or the way that you do. With self-knowledge and college knowledge, everyone gets a best college, even if what's best for you is different from what's best for everyone else. In fact, it's supposed to be that way.

At this time of year, it's easy to think it's gonna take a miracle to get into college. You've worked too hard to believe in things that you don't understand. Instead, remember what home means to you and stay focused on what you've learned about college and yourself, and your college applications will go flying out the door so quickly, you'll realize the miracle is you.

So open up the laptop and pass the Cocoa Doodles. You can do this.

CHAPTER 35

Changing Your Schedule to Include AP Pickleball? Think Again!

It's now the start of senior year. A new locker, a new schedule, and a new background for all your online classes. Awesome!

But wait. You've just looked at your schedule, and you're sure it's a mistake. AP this, Advanced that, Honors something or other. This looks way too hard to make room for fun in your *senior year*.

So, you immediately go into the seven stages of senioritis:

Shock: Whoa! Look at this schedule!

Denial: Who put this schedule together? Not me!

Anger: This reeks! I'm not going to have time to do anything but study.

Bargaining: Wait, it's not too late to change my classes. Maybe I can pick up some easier classes, like Taylor Swift: Fact or Fiction?

Depression: But if I do that, I'll never get into college.

Testing: But maybe I can change just a couple of classes and still be OK.

Now that you're on the road to acceptance—and the road to your counselor's office—you need to ask yourself two questions:

If I drop this class, how strong is the rest of my schedule? When colleges look at your senior year schedule, they want to know you are taking the most challenging classes you can handle without taking on too much. As you think about your class load and how much homework you can handle, remember that strength of schedule is one of the most important parts of the college application. If you're thinking about dropping your only advanced class (and colleges usually have lists of your school's advanced classes), or if you're thinking about dropping an academic class for a nonacademic class, don't do anything until you talk with your counselor.

If I keep this class, will I be able to earn good grades in my other classes? In a perfect world, you would take the most demanding classes in every subject, but realistically, the number of folks who should do that is incredibly small. It's better to think about what happens if you keep this class. Do your grades in your other classes suffer? A B- in an AP class really doesn't help your GPA, or the college's impression of you, all that much if the grades in your other classes went from the A range to the B- range. Challenge yourself? Sure. Drive yourself crazy? Why?

Whatever you decide to do, remember, if you give a college a list of senior year classes, and that list changes in any way, *it is your responsibility to notify that college of the change immediately.* There are some colleges that don't care if you drop AP Chinese for AP Dodgeball. Other colleges do, and failing to tell them your schedule has changed can lead them to cancel your admission. Use your best judgment before and after you change your schedule.

The goal is to make senior year challenging and fun without making it impossible. That's the key to a rich life, and the key to the best kind of college preparation.

One more thing: Sometimes your school's schedule is built in a way that makes it impossible for you to take all the challenging classes you'd like. If that's the case, make sure you tell your counselor, who can mention this to the colleges in their letter about you. It's vital the colleges know that's not your fault.

CHAPTER 36

Lining Up an Interview

Many colleges require letters of recommendation, but very few require an interview. Most students breathe a sigh of relief when they hear this, and I don't know why—after all, why wouldn't you want someone at the college of your dreams to hear about your dreams?

You can fulfill this requirement in one of two ways. You can have the interview on campus, which is nice because you get to see the place you're applying to, a must if at all possible. If you get an on-campus interview, it likely will be with someone who will read your application, so that's a plus as well.

The other way to get an interview is off-campus, of course. This is typically done with a graduate of the college who lives in your community, although more and more off-campus interviews are now being run by admissions officers. These interviewers are trained by the college, so they know how to conduct an interview, while offering insights on what it's like to go to the college as a student, and to talk about what going to the college means to them as an adult.

If you want to interview on campus, you typically have to call the college. These slots usually fill up quickly, so call in July. If the college requires an interview and you can't make it to campus, the local alumni will call you to arrange the meeting. Many more of the local meetings are now being conducted online or by phone, so don't worry if it's not an in-person session.

If you get a message that the college wants to set up an interview, make sure to return the call right away—no later than within twenty-four hours. Work out a time that's good for both of you; the alumni rep knows you are a busy senior, so they will be flexible as long as you let them know when you can meet. In-person interviews should be conducted in a public place (like a coffee shop). If it's an online or phone interview, make sure you set it up to keep all distractions out of the room (no little brothers, parents, or multitasking). If it's a phone interview, try to use a landline.

Confirm the key information the day before the interview by calling the interviewer directly. If you have to leave a message, tell them you're looking forward to seeing them tomorrow at two at the place you'll be meeting, and include your phone number. This shows both courtesy and organization on your part, and colleges like both.

OK, now the big question: what to wear? Because this is a college interview and not a fashion show, you don't have to devote hours to this. Just look nice, and you should be fine. If "nice" suggests you should be a little on the conservative side, you're getting the idea. Typically, guys wear a collared shirt with khakis or dark slacks and something other than sandals or sneakers. Earrings for guys is a tough call—there are some places that aren't crazy about them—and body piercings for everyone tend to still be a no. If you feel strongly this is just about being you, you're welcome to wear them, but know that they still cause a stir in some interview circles.

For females, this means a nonrevealing top and slacks or a knee-length skirt, along with shoes that complement the outfit. Having said all of this, I know many students who have had great interviews wearing a T-shirt and jeans. That approach isn't recommended, but it can work.

Get lots of sleep the night before. All-nighters before a test might be helpful, but all-nighters only make you look tired for an interview, and that doesn't go well for anyone.

CHAPTER 37

Showtime

You've confirmed the date, the time, and the location, and you don't look like you just got out of bed. Excellent.

For a face-to-face interview, arrive at least five minutes ahead of time. This gives you a chance to catch your breath, get comfortable with the location, and use the restroom if you need to. If you get lost, *call* if you can. Getting lost is not a reason for being denied admission, but being gracious about getting lost is the right thing to do and demonstrates your respect for the interviewer. If the interviewer arrives after you do, stand up, offer your hand, and smile.

The key to any interview is to just be yourself, really. The interviewer will probably ask you open-ended questions—questions where you'll have to respond with something more than just "yes" or "no." Typical questions include "Why are you interested in our college?"…"What are you most proud of in high school?"…and the famous "Tell me about yourself." Your answers should be complete and about a minute long. Make sure you answer the question—no ducking—and show grace, warmth, and maybe a little humor in your answers. Don't go overboard on the humor, and show your personal side, but don't get too personal. If you want to share a story you used as part of a college essay, that's more than OK. It's likely the interviewer hasn't read your application yet, but make sure to add to the story since you don't want to simply replicate your application.

If you're having an interview that isn't required, you're going to have to take charge of the interview a little more. You had to have a reason to ask for the interview, so make that clear right away. If you had unusual circumstances that affected your life in high school (illness, family issues), talk briefly about them, but spend more time talking about how you overcame them and the lessons you've learned from the experience. If you have additional questions about the college, fire away, but do make sure they can't be answered somewhere on the college's website. If you're there to show interest in the college, talk about why you like the place and what you think you have to give to the place. The idea is to take charge while being gracious, to give the meeting substance without being lengthy, and to show the interviewer why the college can't live without you. Keep these things in mind, and you'll be great.

In all interviews, you'll be asked if you have questions. It's good to have one or two questions in mind in advance. If you happen to come up with questions on the spot, that's OK too, but the last thing you want to do is have no questions at all. These questions should require answers that aren't on the college website or in admissions material, since the quality of the questions shows how interested you are in the school. You can also ask an alumni interviewer about their perceptions of the college. The answer you get is just their perspective, but it's a good way to connect, and it's great information to have as you continue to shape your ideas about the college.

Stand up and shake hands when the face-to-face interview is over; for all interviews, thank the interviewer, then off you go. It is exceptionally good form to call or email the interviewer the next day to thank them again and to encourage them to contact you if they have any questions. I'm a little old school about this, so I think a handwritten note is even better, but you might not have their address. Either way, make sure you show your gratitude for the chance to talk with them, and all will be well.

CHAPTER 38

Essays

I don't know why students freak about essays—they're all about you. Students spend hours on social media talking about themselves and what they think about, but have a college ask you about your favorite place to be, and all you can say is "The library. Look at all those books."

That's too bad, because colleges want to hear what you think, and they want you to be you. Most colleges give you a very general topic to write on, where you get to steer the ship. If they give you a question on a more specific topic, you can still answer it in a way that shows them who you really are. This isn't algebra; this is you.

Here are some general guidelines:

Answer the question. It's great to answer a question with lots of broad background, but if they want to know about a person who inspired you, tell them. If they get to the end of your answer and still don't know, you've just given the college a reason to reject you. This isn't Washington, DC, so don't obfuscate.

Answer the question honestly. Don't say your father just because you think you're supposed to, and don't say Mario just to be cute. The essay is a guided tour of your mind, life, vision, and soul—what you are, not what you think you're supposed to be. Show them the real deal.

Watch the humor. An Ivy League rep once said if you could get him to laugh out loud when he read your essay, you were in. Trouble is, lots of people try and fail. What's funny to you may be trite, dull, pathetic, or strange to someone else. It's usually best to leave the humor to the people in the comedy clubs.

Watch the content. Trite (an essay on what you should write the essay about), pathetic ("I'm not worthy to be admitted, but take me anyway"), common (sports as a life lesson), sappy (anything about breaking up with a love interest), or just plain strange ("I'm actually a vampire") should be avoided. Your writing should be an honest look at you, but it needs to be fresh. This is an introduction, not the tenth week of therapy. Be focused and balanced, and you'll do fine.

Show it to an English teacher who knows you. At least one friendly English teacher understands this is a personal essay, not a book report, so they won't give it the usual red pen treatment. Since they also know the rules of grammar, this is your new best friend. Bring them your rough draft and lots of chocolate, and let the games begin.

Write the essay yourself. The essay is a guided tour of your life, written by you. Having someone else "significantly edit" your essay is your first encounter with college-level plagiarism, and it may be your last. Forty-five-year-old parents write differently than seventeen-year-old students, and colleges know this. Don't do it.

Repeat yourself. You can use the same essay for questions from different colleges, as long as the essay still answers the question and shows something about you. Make *sure* to change the names of any colleges you use in the essay (Don't tell Lawrence University, "I've always wanted to go to Valparaiso"), and make sure you include information specific to the college ("I love how the Butler Bulldog lives in the campus bookstore"), and you should be fine.

Write only on the weekends. Weekdays are for school, studying, and living your life—plus, essays written at ten o'clock Tuesday night after three hours of homework are always pretty bad. Aim to complete one set of essays every weekend, and you'll be fine.

Colleges would love to have you on campus for two weeks to get to really know you, but if they did that with every applicant, you'd be forty-five before they decided if they could admit you. The essay takes the place of those two weeks. As a wise admissions officer once said, write it so that when they look up from reading it, they're surprised you aren't in the room with them.

CHAPTER 39

Essays Part Two— the Four Ds and More

Whenever I talk to college admissions officers—the people who read the essays you write—I ask them for advice I can pass along to students. Year after year, they say the essays are the best chance for students to show the colleges who they are and what they sound like. Both are a key part to a successful application.

To my surprise, the reps often have some don'ts to pass along as well, including things in student essays that just don't work. I'm passing these along to make sure they aren't part of your application. This is the kind of attention you *don't* want to get.

Avoid the four Ds. Essays on negative life events can be very tricky. Unless enough time has passed since the experience occurred, the essay can be too personal, too much of a rant, or just plain hard to read. One rep said that, in general, students should avoid the four Ds—drugs, dating, death, and divorce—but you get the idea. If you want to write about a personal challenge, emphasize what you learned through the situation and how you grew. If you dwell on the experience itself, the essay will not achieve its purpose.

It's not a book report. You may indeed think *Lord of the Flies* was the best book ever written, but there's a point where talking about the book becomes more academic (and about the book) than personal (about you). If you're writing about your response to the book or how it influenced your life, the right writing ratio is a lot less about the book and way more about you. Once again, it's all about you.

Grandma Barbara isn't going to college. "Less is more" is also the rule when the question asks you to talk about someone you admire. It's great that your hero was born in Scotland and learned the bagpipes at age four, but that kind of detail leaves less words for the college to hear about what you've done with the inspiration that person has given you—and that's the story they want to hear.

It's OK to go on and on about Granny B if she's applying to college, too; if she isn't, a few specifics and qualities will nicely set the stage for you to talk about what she's done and ways she's made a difference in you and the way you see the world. That's the main entrée on the menu of the college essay. Let the reps dig into a generous portion.

Additional information can be a beautiful thing. One rep pointed out that most college applications have a space where applicants can include information the college needs to know. The additional information box can be the place where you explain how you got ill in tenth grade, when you moved in the middle of junior year, why a summer school grade is still incomplete, and more. They don't need to be part of an essay if you have other things to say.

Good essays are like cheese—let them age. Once you're done with an essay, hit Save and let it sit for two days. You'll be amazed at the small changes you see that need to be made just by leaving the essays alone for a while.

CHAPTER 40

The "Challenges" Essay

Essay topics change from year to year and from college to college, but one that always shows up is "Describe a challenge you have faced and how you overcame it."

If the topic itself seems like a challenge, keep these points in mind:

The goal of the essay is for the colleges to learn more about you. Essays are your opportunity to show the colleges the person behind the grades and the numbers. Effective essays show them (not tell them) a story, give them a taste of your voice and a peek at the way you look at the world, and show them your ability to write.

A challenge isn't always a crisis. A "setback" or "adversity" certainly can involve a serious situation, but challenges aren't always life threatening. They almost always give you something new to think about, but that's different—and often not that dire. Wake-up calls come in different ringtones—talk about one that really got you thinking, and don't worry if it didn't involve falling off Mount Everest.

Some challenges may be too personal. Generally speaking, boyfriend/girlfriend breakups are out; try as they might, most students can't write about these without sounding too wounded or too bitter. The same is true for addictions; you are moving on beautifully with your life, but talking about the experience is usually one of the last skills you gain. It's always a good idea to show your essays to your counselor, but if you're writing about a personal issue, this is a must. It might be better for the counselor to address this issue in their letter rather than you doing so in your essay.

Watch the overused and the cheesy. Athletics is indeed a life-changing experience for many students. It's also one of the most used topics in college essays and has been for about fifty years—and that makes it tired. Try as you may, it's unlikely you will say anything about "sports as a metaphor for life" the rep hasn't already read a dozen times that day. It may mean a lot to you, but it's not going to make you memorable. Strongly consider another topic.

The other topic to avoid here is "the challenge I overcame coming up with an answer to this essay." Like writing about what to write about, this approach almost always comes across as an "I love me" message, and that's not what colleges want to see. Keep thinking.

Don't skimp on the resolution and reflection. It's good to give a clear picture of what you were facing, but dwelling too long on the problem doesn't show the college how you resolved it, or what you think about the experience now that it's behind you (or if it's behind you). Colleges want to hear about an important life lesson you've learned, and the finale is more important than the overture. Don't overlook it.

Like all essays, write this one yourself. Too much "help" on an essay makes it sound like someone else wrote it because someone else did. That leaves you with nowhere to go next fall. Talk about adversity.

Another challenge is when a college asks for a minimum number of words in an essay but doesn't give a maximum. This creates a situation where you are likely to overwrite, something common in essays. You're writing something nice about Grandma Barbara, and suddenly you're describing her trip last summer to Niagara Falls. You're officially in over your head.

The key to making sure this doesn't happen is professional help. Show your essays to an English teacher who likes you. Their careful mix of compassion and expertise will give you the help you need to tell the colleges what they need to know without pushing them to the point of boredom, madness—or rejecting you because you can't get to the point. English teachers are busy people, so ask ahead, set up an appointment, and bring armloads of chocolate.

Yes, I did say armloads.

CHAPTER 41

The "Why Us" Essay

Another essay many colleges have students write asks them to share what they know about the college. Since most colleges let you apply online, it's pretty easy to complete the application, as you now know. For some colleges, that means they get far more applicants than they can admit. In fact, the number one reason for most admission denials at these colleges has nothing to do with the student; it happens because the college runs out of room before they run out of qualified applicants (more on that later).

To help them sort out the seriously interested students from the students who were cruising the web and thought, "Hey, why not," many colleges ask what's called the "Why Us" question. The exact wording varies from college to college, but the basic question boils down to this: What have you learned about our college in particular that makes you think it can help you grow, challenge you, and be a place where you can give back to the community?" Here's a pretty typical version of the Why Us question:

"How does the University of Chicago, as you know it now, satisfy your desire for a particular kind of learning, community, and future? Please address with some specificity your own wishes and how they relate to UChicago."

A strong response to the Why Us question has two key parts:

Start by talking about you. Most Why Us questions are asked in a way that makes the student think they should start their answer with a laundry list of everything they know about the college—the programs, the campus, the mascot, and even the football team, especially if the team is nationally ranked.

You want to take a fresher approach. Since most students are going to start their answer talking about the college, your response should start with you. "Ever since I was young, I was interested in listening to people and what they had to say. That interest has led to many adventures in my life—strong friendships, volunteer opportunities on helplines, running counseling groups at school. I've long believed I was put on this earth to serve, and I'm grateful my school and community have given me those opportunities."

This is a great start to an essay for several reasons. First, it's about you, not the college. That's going to be enough all by itself to get the attention of any reader, since it isn't a list about the attributes of the school. Second, it gives you a chance to briefly highlight your extracurriculars. These are by no means the start of the show, but they are evidence to support your opening statement.

The reader is now wondering exactly where this is going, since you have yet to talk about the college.

CHAPTER 42

The "Why Us" Essay, Part Two

Now that you have their attention...

Talk about the college second. Following up with a narrative of what you know about the college now tells them, "I know who I am and what I want. This is why your college is the place for me to be in the fall." Again, this isn't a list of the college's attributes—they already know what programs they offer. Instead, this is your perceptions of the school and how the two of you fit together. Something like this:

"That's why University of Chicago is such a great place for me to be. The school's social work program is steeped in hands-on learning experiences in clinics and other programs. This means I'll be able to continue helping others while I learn even more about how to help others. The student-led organizations (especially the Community and Economic Development Organization) offer me a chance to learn and contribute to the well-being of my peers, and Chicago's well-known core curriculum will help me understand more about the world, especially the segments I have yet to experience firsthand."

This answer shows the student has researched the college beyond just the first few web pages and has found many things they're interested in. Just as important—and this is a game-changer—this answer addresses what the student will give to the college in turn as an engaged member of the community. It's too easy for the Why Us question to sound like "gimme gimme gimme." Talking in specific ways about what you have to offer the college is something few students do effectively and can make all the difference.

Two other things about this essay: First, many colleges put a very short limit to the Why Us question. Often, it's 150 words, and at one college, it's 125 *characters*. For some reason, that gives students the impression the answer is less important to the college.

Nope. In some cases, this is the question admissions officers read *first*-- and if they don't like what they see, you're on your way to a No. The brief size of the response likely means this will actually be the essay you work on most. Start with a big answer, then edit away.

Second, don't think you can use the same Why Us answer for more than one college. Unlike some other essays, if you try to submit your Why Us answer to more than one school, you're going to leave out an important level of detail for either answer—or both. When you think you're done with a Why Us answer, read it, and ask yourself, "Could I submit this answer to another college?" If so, it's time to start over.

CHAPTER 43

The Final Check

Now that the essays are done, you're in the home stretch. Here are a few final touches:

- Almost every college has a secondary school report that asks for a counselor recommendation, a transcript, or both. If you gave your counselor's email address on an online application, you should be all set; if not, these forms go to your counselor *at least* a month before they are due. Check your school's policy to make sure you turn them in on time, fill out the information at the top (making sure to sign the FERPA waiver), and hand them in. If the college wants your grades from the first part of senior year, they'll give you a form for that as well. Be sure to turn that in, too.

- I'm hoping you checked your transcript for missing or incorrect grades when you met with your counselor junior year. If not, check now—that D you seem to have earned in algebra might not be your best friend right now.

- Plan ahead. Complete your applications in the order they are due, not by how many parts they have. This means rolling admissions apps are first, November 1st apps are next, and January 1st apps are last.

January 1st apps are especially tricky. On the one hand, the deadline gives you the December break to work on the applications, but you'll be doing that without the help of your school counselor, who is also on break.

There is no circumstance under which you are to call your counselor over break. If you haven't picked up on this yet, counselors are run ragged when school is in session, putting in twelve-hour days on a regular basis. Their break isn't so much a break as it is a chance to restore, and they need that time. Unless your school policy says to turn them in earlier, your counselor forms should get to your counselor absolutely no later than December 1. If you add a college at the last minute, or run into an application problem over break, go ahead and submit the application, then email your counselor to let them know what's going on. They won't respond until after break, but most colleges will gladly take your counselor's call and help fix whatever issue might arise—as long as the application has been submitted on time.

- Never mail the day an application is due. If you have to mail anything to a college, make sure it gets in the mail a day or two before the actual deadline. For January 1st applications, you have no choice but to mail early, since post offices are closed on New Year's Day. But life has a funny way of clogging up your schedule on days things have to be postmarked. Again, plan ahead.

After a day or two of resting from application frenzy, it's time to move on—either on to the next application or back to the life of the living. Waiting to hear from a college is like waiting to be asked out—the longer you spend time just waiting for it to happen, the longer it seems to take. You have six months of senior year left, so there's plenty on your senior bucket list you're dying to get to. Jump in.

In addition, don't look back. As a ninth grader, you wanted perfect grades, smoked SATs, universal acclaim as the Ruler of Community Service, and an acceptance letter from Dream School U framed in gold. Maybe you got those things, and maybe you didn't. Either way, if the last app is submitted and you've done everything you can to make it all work, the only thing left to do is what you were always doing—make the most of every learning and living opportunity, and enjoying all of them for what you can give and learn from them.

Finally, if you hear back from a college saying they are missing a part of your application, do not panic, and do not yell at your counselor. This happens all the time, and the reason the college is telling you is so you can help them get it to them. Contact the right person (teacher, counselor, you) and get it in right away. This is a do-over, and you get those. It's more than OK.

CHAPTER 44

For Parents—Before You Yell at Your School Counselor

This is one of only two chapters devoted exclusively to parents. Students who like to make sure their parents are being as helpful as possible should also read this chapter. You'd be amazed how ordinarily calm parents can lose it under certain circumstances.

You've worked so hard to schedule, prepare, and nudge your high school senior to apply to college on time. You shared that small thrill when they hit Submit with time to spare, and you thought you were all set.

Until they got the email.

"Our records indicate your application is incomplete. Unless we receive a copy of your high school transcript in the next five days, we will be unable to process your application."

At this point, you've decided this is personal, so even though it's seven o'clock at night, you pick up the phone and leave the Mother of All Voice Mails for your school counselor.

Boy, did you just blow it. Here's why:

Your entire reaction is based on a wrong assumption. The college hasn't said, "Forget it"; they've said, "We need something." You can help them get what they need. Was that voice mail helping the college? Was it helping your child?

The college likely has the information. Even with advanced technology, admissions offices get backed up, so the transcript might not be in your child's file, but it is in the college's application system somewhere. That means your high school counselor—the one you just called incompetent—sent the transcript, and in a timely fashion.

If the college already has one copy of your child's transcript, they don't want another one. If the transcript is already in the college's system, they really don't want a second copy, since that would just increase their backlog. The only way to double-check is for someone to call the admissions office and see if the first copy has found its way to your child's file.

You just berated the person who can help you the most. To be honest, the person who should call the college is your child (it's their application), but it's likely you want the school counselor to call. You know, the one you just described as incapable of doing their job.

This isn't to say they won't help you and give your child their full support, but if you've just given them a big, and very angry, piece of your mind, you've now put them in a spot where they need to start keeping a paper trail of your, um, complaint. That takes time; so does recovering from being told by someone who last applied to college twenty years ago that you don't know what you're doing. You want the problem resolved now, but you've just prevented that from happening. Is that really a good idea?

You've just left an impression you can't erase. Let's say the transcript is already there, or that a second one is sent, making your child's file complete. The college is now considering your child carefully, but they'd like a little more information about them. How does your child react to setbacks? How well do they speak up for themselves? Do they demonstrate flexibility?

The person the college will be talking to is—you guessed it—the school counselor, who is now only able to extol the virtues of your child's ability to hand their problems over to Mommy and Daddy to solve, simply because that's what the counselor has experienced. This isn't about a grudge; this is about their experience.

It's easy to freak out about the college admissions process, but just because you can, it doesn't mean you should. That's even truer when challenges arise, and your child looks to you to set the model for handling adversity they should take with them to college. This assumes the college still wants them. Part of that is up to you.

CHAPTER 45

Second-Guessing Your List? Guess Again

Late October can be a challenging time to apply to college. You've already applied to a couple of colleges, and now you're swimming in more applications and essays. You're starting to wonder if this is all really worth it, when along comes an email with happy news from a college you applied to in September. Congratulations, you're in!

You have now entered the Goldilocks zone. (Remember her? If not, go ahead and look her up). Right now, you think your list is:

Too hard. With five class papers to write and the fall play, you're sure you're applying to too many colleges. You only did in-depth research on half of them, but the time you're spending on essays would be better spent if you were keeping your grades up. Plus, you're already admitted to college. Do you really need more?

Too soft. Sure, you're in at one college, but that was a likely school. In fact, every school you're applying to looks like a sure thing. Maybe it's time to ramp things up—and if that means writing more essays at Grandma's over Thanksgiving, you're all for it.

These feelings may seem to be opposites, but they are signs of the same thing: you are freaking out about applying to college. Pull up a bowl of porridge, and we can sort this out in three easy questions:

How did you feel about your college list in September? If you put a lot of thought into your choices and researched all the colleges, chances are you'd be cutting out some good options by cutting down the list. The busy-ness of school is blocking your view, and it's time to take a breath.

On the other hand, if you threw your list together to get Mom and Dad off your back, you may now have a better idea of what you want in a college, or don't want. If that's the case, you have time to revisit the list and good reason to do so.

How many essays do you really have left? Count up the essays you have left to write. Now divide that number by six. That's the number of essays you need to complete each weekend to be finished with your apps by mid-December—and that's the goal. If you mix and match short and long essays, you're probably OK if you have to complete three essays each weekend, maybe four. (And remember, no writing essays during the school week. That's the time for schoolwork and for keeping those grades up.)

Then again, if you have to write one-sixth of an essay every weekend, there's room to add to the list. Write down what you're looking for in a college, and spend part of this weekend looking around for more good matches. It's clear you can let the essays rest for now.

Have your college goals changed since September? If you have new college plans, a review of the list is absolutely the right thing to do. If all of the colleges you have on the list now are keepers, it's time to pull up your socks and do the heavy lifting of the essays. Persisting now will be good practice for college, when you'll have to choose between turning in your paper on time and the euchre tournament.

Goldilocks made bad choices—trespassing, destruction of private property, and napping after a big meal. Don't let this happen to you. Step back, think about what matters most to you, and you'll make a decision about apps that's just right.

CHAPTER 46

Making It Through the Holidays without Being Broken

Completing college applications can be hard work, work that often runs through the holiday season. Since everyone else is taking some time off, this would seem to be the perfect opportunity to hang out with your family, especially since this could be your last Thanksgiving/New Year/Kwanzmasakah as a full-time occupant of your parents' home. How could this possibly be a bad idea?

"My friend," says you, "you clearly don't know my parents, or my Uncle Bob."

Fair enough; it's time to take back the holidays. Here are the three keys to thriving (not just surviving) this wonderful season senior year:

Treat Uncle Bob like you and he are adults. If you're smart enough to go to college, you're smart enough to sort out how Uncle Bob operates—and that's the key to success. Once he's through updating you on his thriving business and gloating about the political party of his choice, he's going to put a large piece of turkey on his fork and ask, "So, how's the college hunt going?"

You're now thinking, "This is the end." You haven't heard from the college that was supposed to decide in October, and your other colleges are small schools Uncle Bob hasn't heard of. Heck, *you* hadn't even heard of them until last year.

And this, my friend, makes a wonderful foundation for your response.

"Well, Uncle Bob, I applied to Eastnorthern State U, and I thought of you when I answered the essays, since you've told me how much you love the school. I guess everybody's uncle feels that way because the college is weeks behind in admissions decisions, but I should hear by Super Bowl.

"I know Mom has told you about my other schools, where some of the students major in the History of Haiku and take classes like Fruit Leather in a Modern Society. I won't hear from them until spring, but if I decide to attend one of them, I'll be sure to bring a flare gun with me to campus, in case they try to force-feed me tofu."

At this point, Uncle Bob will look at you, chuckle a little, and then go back to talking about the glory, or evils, of Ronald Wilson Reagan.

Welcome to adulthood.

Your applications and Black Saturday. The next holiday hurdle is the Saturday after Thanksgiving (or Christmas or...) when even the adults are ready for a break from each other. This is typically the time when your parents—who love you—will say, "Honey, Uncle Bob is going out to lunch with us. Don't you think this would be a good time to work on your college essays?"

This requires preparation. Put together a spreadsheet ahead of time with the name of every college you're applying to, the date each application is due, and the date you will work on that application. Print out a copy and keep it in your back pocket, saving it for this moment when you open it with a modest flourish, hand it to your parents, and say, "I've got it covered. Have a great lunch."

And as you put your earphones back on to fall under the spell of Spotihideandseek, you will see your parents weep with amazement and joy. Their widdle baby is all grown up.

Remember the reason for the season. You have parents who love you, an Uncle Bob who is the lovable kind of crazy, and a world of possibilities awaiting you in college. If ever there was a time for gratitude, it is now.

So head over the river and through the woods with confidence, you college slayer.

CHAPTER 47

Scholarship Essays in Six Hundred Words or Less

Happy New Year! How you doing, senior? Had a good holiday? Back at school? Great!

Ready to write some scholarship essays?

Yeah, yeah, I figured you'd say that. The keyboard calluses from your application essays are finally beginning to fade, and along I come to remind you of an essential point: you still can't go to college if you don't have the money.

So it's time to do some scholarship essays.

Go to a scholarship search site—I like finaid.org, but check with your counselor—and look for scholarships that meet your hobbies, interests, and background. You also should check on the websites of your colleges, but you're going to be considered for most of those scholarships just by applying for admission. If you need a separate application for a particular scholarship, the website will tell you that.

Next, scope out your high school website, or ask your counselor about the list of local scholarships that are available. This is the most neglected pot of scholarship money because most people think the $200 to $500 scholarships from the local VFW or Kiwanis Club aren't all that big. Fair enough, but if it takes you an hour to write an essay for a $200 scholarship, that means you're making $200 an hour. That's a little more than you'd make at a local burger spot.

You should also remember that local scholarships have a much smaller pool of applicants. The scholarships you see on national sites draw national attention; if you're going to the only high school in town, you may be one of three applicants for the Good Citizen scholarship.

Once you hit these sites, look for scholarships that have a common theme. A number of scholarships center on patriotism, for example, so you could probably use the same essay (or tweak it) to apply for all of these scholarships and be a serious contender for each one. If you pull in three of these scholarships, your hour of writing is now worth $600 an hour. Nice, huh?

You'll also want to ask your counselor if you can fill out one application for all of the local scholarships. Counselors know students are only going to apply for so many scholarships, and they also know the VFW will get discouraged if only three students apply for their scholarship. One application that covers all local scholarships keeps both groups happy—more students apply, and those students can apply with less work. Easy.

Another option is to see if any of the essays you wrote for admission will work for a scholarship. It's more than OK to do this, as long as the essay truly answers the scholarship question. If not, some of them may inspire you to write something great, but different, for the scholarships.

You'll also want to take one more look at your college list and think about the cost of each school. It's way too easy to get caught up in admit letters in April that come with financial aid packages that require you to take out loans that will cost more than a Lamborghini. Instead of being shocked, however, you find yourself saying, "Oh, I love this school so much, I'll just find a way to pay for it."

It's certainly true money can come from unexpected places, but when your college payment options boil down to starting out your work life with a student loan the size of two car payments or hitting the Powerball, applying for scholarships now seems like a smart thing to do. It is.

CHAPTER 48

I Love You, You're Perfect—Now Go Study

It might seem early to talk about this, but there are recent reports seniors are starting to slack off in their studies as early as November of their twelfth grade year. Known as "senioritis," this mental vacation doesn't usually start until April, when the sun is out, graduation is in sight, and a young person's fancy turns to—well, not school.

It's easy to see why so many students succumb to senioritis. It's not that you don't care about school as much as you need a break from reading, writing, and thinking—at least long enough to really take in the idea that your time in this school, with these friends, is coming to an end. Add in a little holiday stress from well-meaning relatives about your college plans, and it's easy to see why you feel this way. What you need is a little understanding, a few words of encouragement—and a kick in the earbuds.

I know, I know, I'm supposed to be the caring counselor. Truth is, I am. I understand colleges are saying maybe to more students than ever before, so they'll want to see the grades you earned in the first part of senior year, and sometimes the grades you're earning in the spring of senior year. With increases in the number of students applying to college, there are more students applying for the same number of seats—and, in some cases, for fewer seats. This means colleges are getting more applications from students with strong grades, allowing them to be a little fussier and take a closer look at each applicant.

It's true that this is your last winter concert, spring sports season, and prom. It's also true that the grades you get during senior year can be the difference in the offers of admission you get and the ones you get to keep—get it?

Going into cruise control now is like saying the four-foot putt you have left doesn't matter since you've already hit the ball four hundred yards. Every golfer knows that just isn't the case—if it ain't in the hole, the match isn't won.

So enjoy senior year but also do what you need to do to stay college ready. Pull up the home page of Dream School U to remember your goal, paint your nails highlighter yellow to help you study, have your parents hide your QBox 2563 until you've studied for two hours every night—whatever it takes to make it to the finish line.

Colleges read your application to discover the student you've been, and many ask to see the student you currently are. The answer they get isn't blowing in the wind; it's going to be written in the essay of the life you're going to live from now until graduation day. So keep your skills sharp, continue to contribute to your community, and learn a few things that will make the transition to college a smooth one.

Finally, remember your schedule. We've already talked about the dangers of changes. Just remember that if you do make a change, you have to tell every college you apply to about the change. That's also true if you decide to make your schedule harder, since it's to your advantage to tell them you're taking your game to a new level.

That's your academic game, not your game on the QBox 2563.

CHAPTER 49

A Word about Grade Grubbing: No

In addition to thinking about changing their spring schedules, many seniors will be getting their current grades and realizing the time they spent at the Harry Potter film marathon, combined with a little Thanksgiving senioritis, took their toll on recent grades.

"A B+ in physics?"

"A C-minus in Business Law?"

"A *what* in English?"

Welcome to grade-groveling season, the time when parents across America look at their seniors' laundry and say, "What are the stains on the knees of these pants, and how did they get there?"

From buttering up to begging, from outrage to despair, seniors will spend the next couple of weeks planning, scheming, and hoping they can squeeze just one little grade bump from three or four teachers, largely because they are certain college will take one look at these grades and say, "Yeah, well, no."

I suppose this is where I'm supposed to offer words of solace and encouragement, and suggest some approaches toward importunacy that will succeed. OK, here goes:

Good luck with that.

I know you feel badly, much like the point guard who sinks the winning shot after the buzzer sounds, or the junior who understands the writing prompt on the English midterm on their drive home from school. This isn't easy to live with, and you were so close, but it just didn't happen.

"But college is on the line," says you, "and I can fix this because time isn't up. I'm still in high school, and I have the same teacher."

True enough, but look at the calendar. It's a different marking period, and this grade was for last marking period. On the time-space continuum, the jig is up—and if you don't understand that, maybe you really deserved that low physics grade. Just sayin'.

If that's not enough to get your head out of the rearview mirror, remember that a small bump in one class grade—say, from a B to a B+—raises your GPA by about .008. Combine that with the advice more than one college rep has given me—"One grade alone will not sink a college application"—and I'd say it's time to leave your teachers in peace.

This leads me to my last point:

Unlike Aunt Midge's home knit socks, grades aren't gifts given by someone else—they are earned by you. If you have reason to believe your grade was calculated incorrectly, follow the grade appeal process outlined in the student handbook.

At the same time, I'm guessing this process has nothing to do with baking cookies for your teacher, following them to the parking lot at the end of the day, or having your parents "accidentally" bump into them at the grocery store—and it really has nothing to do with saying, "But a grade this low will keep me out of college."

From what I know, that isn't true, and even if it is, the person who gave you that "gift" of a grade isn't looking at you from the teacher's desk third period. They are looking at you from the bathroom mirror every morning.

Believe me when I tell you I'm feelin' it for you, but it's time to pull up those socks Aunt Midge gave you and move on...because one low grade may not keep you from being admitted, but a couple more low grades this marking period can put you on the fast track to having a college admission offer taken away. It happens all the time.

There's nothing you can do if you fell behind, but it's now time to spring ahead.

CHAPTER 50

Twenty-Minute Meetings, To Be Continued

To review the last few chapters: There is no letting up on taking tough classes, no giving up on writing essays, no slacking off on homework, and no telling the teachers how smart they are in the hopes your B will magically become an A.

Fair enough, you think. At least you can stop meeting with your parents each week now that the college choices are all made.

Yes. About that.

It would seem something has happened since you first carved twenty minutes out of your week to talk with your parents about college. To begin with, they've learned to give you space; most parents think it's crazy to limit themselves to twenty minutes a week to talk about college, especially during the weeks in the fall when you were working on applications and telling them absolutely nothing beyond their allotted time. They've learned to trust you more, which will come in handy over time like when you go to college, when you buy your first couch, and when you name your first child after a *Game of Thrones* character.

But something else has happened. Because you met once each week when no one was rushing to get you anywhere, your parents had a chance to see what you've made of yourself since the last time things weren't so crazy—which for most families is when you were about four. I have to tell you, they really liked what they saw. And they'd like to keep seeing it every week for twenty minutes.

This probably makes no sense to you, but when you came home and said, "Last winter exam! Yes!" they said, "Last winter exam? No!" They told you they cried when you went to this year's Sadie Hawkins Dance because they thought you looked nice, right? Nope, because it was the last one. And remember how they once dreaded having you home from school for any reason? Not so much now.

Through the twenty-minute meetings, your parents realize they have a child who is smart, knows who they are, and understands a little about how the world works—and that child is moving out of the house in six months. Giving you up then is something they'll figure out; giving you up now is something they would just as soon not do.

Of course, you don't have to talk about college. Now is not the time to sit in the living room, holding hands and listening to the cuckoo clock chirp away until the college decisions arrive. Order in some food, catch up on a movie, work a jigsaw puzzle—do something, do anything together.

Love is as much a verb as it is a noun, and showing them what you feel at a time of uncertainty (for you and them) can make a memory that will last far longer than whatever East Coast U has to say in a couple of weeks.

No college decision will change the way they feel about you, just like it shouldn't change the way you feel about yourself. Twenty weekly minutes of meeting time that isn't required will bring that home as nothing else can, and build a stronger base for whatever is waiting after Decision Day.

Give it some thought as you work on your next scholarship essay. They're sure thinking about it—they've told me as much.

CHAPTER 51

Understanding Financial Aid Awards

We're talking about financial aid awards before we talk about admissions decisions because things can get a little crazy when colleges start to tell you you're in. So we need to plan ahead.

Award letters can be a little dense, and no two are structured the same way, so comparing them can be challenging. Since paying for college is like buying a new car (or two) every year for four consecutive years, understanding what you're getting into is a must. Here's how:

Read the financial aid award letter five times. Your heart is racing because you're going to follow your parent's footsteps to East Coast College. You (or your parents) have skimmed the award letter twice, and you think you can pay most of what the award letter seems to be saying you have to pay. Not good enough.

Skimming is great, but it's time to celebrate. Put the letter away, order your favorite pizza, and pick up the letter again tomorrow—then again the day after that, then again this weekend. If the letter tells you different things every time you read it, you need some help. This is typical—it still isn't good, but it's typical.

Use the tools. Colleges often send worksheets along with your award letter; some have more information on their website, and some simply say, "Questions? Call us!" This is no time not to ask questions. Use the financial GPS accessories to find out where you are and where you think your bank account is heading.

Call anyway. Even if you *swear* you know what the letter says, use the expertise of the financial aid office to your advantage. If you don't know what to say, try this: "We received my (my child's) acceptance letter, and we're so thrilled to hear the good news, I'm not sure I can completely focus on the award letter. If I read it correctly, they'll receive five thousand in grant money they don't have to pay back, they'll work eight hours a week at an on-campus job, and there's twelve hundred in student loans. Is that right?"

Be quiet, and let them do their job. Once you tell the financial aid office what you see, it's time for them to talk. It's not uncommon for an aid office to pull up your financial aid file and find a better way to package the aid or discover new money that's just become available. They are good at their job, and they want to help you. Listen and let them.

Update them. Your financial picture may have changed dramatically in the two or three months since you filled out the form, or maybe there's part of your financial picture you never had a chance to explain. This happens all the time. Be sure the college knows what's going on, and be prepared to send documentation to support your claims. Nothing may change, but the only way something good might happen is if you tell them.

CHAPTER 52

The Chapter to Read
on March 15

If you've taken any of the advice from these last few chapters, what could have been a winter of discontent waiting to hear from the colleges has instead been filled with writing thoughtful scholarship essays, recommitting your resources to learning, and rediscovering your parents are pretty great people.

But now the winter is passed, and the voice of the college admissions officer can be heard in our land.

This is a time of great excitement for all of you, but before you go any further, it's important to know three things about selective college admissions. I cannot overstate the importance of reading this twice, thoroughly, before you move ahead. OK?

Some colleges will find their applications are at an all-time high. The number of students graduating from high school goes up and down, but one constant is the number of students applying to highly selective colleges: it always tends to go up. Even if it didn't, getting ad-mitted to colleges with a 6 percent acceptance rate is just plain hard to do. This isn't a random process, and there's more to it than just grades, but an increase in the number of applicants makes it that much harder to get admitted.

There is a common reason why colleges deny admission to most applicants. The number one reason selective colleges turn down most applicants is simple: they run out of room before they run out of great applicants. If they had more dorm rooms, and more professors, and more classrooms, they'd love to take more students. But they cannot do justice to the students they admit by taking too many students, since no one gets a quality education that way—and that's not fair to anyone.

An admissions decision is *not* a character indictment. With more applications and limited space, colleges must create a learning com-munity that is exciting, diverse, and rich with opportunities. Doing that is a mix of science and art, a mixture of data (grades, maybe test scores) and insight (essays, letters of recommendation), and frankly, a little guesswork, where (as one admissions officer said) the standard is excellence, not perfection. In selecting these students, these colleges will tell you that just about everyone who applied qualifies for admis-sion—they would be a great student, benefit the college tremendously, and contribute to the college in many ways. Since you applied to a highly selective college, all of that applies to you.

Given that, I can't think of any way a letter of denial or wait list should be interpreted to mean "The college doesn't like me," or worse, "I am not a good person." College admissions is about many things, but it is never a judgment about you as a person.

Most colleges go to great pains to point this out when they send their "no" letters. Believe me when I tell you they aren't just being nice; they truly honor and respect everything you have done as a person, and they are grateful you applied to their college. That may not mean much the minute you hear the news, but it will over time. Whether the college says yes, no, or maybe, your value and worth as a person is cast in stone and can be shaken by absolutely no one, be it another person or an admissions committee.

Your life isn't in that envelope or email; it's just an admissions decision. You already have a life, and a fine one at that.

CHAPTER 53

When a College Says No

The real madness of March has nothing to do with basketball. It begins when colleges announce their admissions decisions, starting around March 20. As a pregame warm-up, let's review what we already know:

- Most selective colleges report an increase in applicants every year.
- Since these schools don't admit more students than they did the previous year, that means they end up saying no to more students…and wait-listing more students.
- This increase means fewer students are likely to be admitted from the wait list come May—and if they are admitted, financial aid will be scarce.

To ease your concern, I have one word of advice. Actually, it's a number: 850

To begin with, calm down. This is not the highest score you can earn on some mystery version of the SAT. Eight hundred fifty is the number of valedictorians recently rejected from one of America's most prestigious colleges. These students represented the best their high schools had to offer, they did everything they were supposed to do, yet they weren't even offered a place on the wait list.

At this point you're probably thinking one of two things:

1. **"Wow, they put in all that work for nothing."**
2. **"Jeez, if they can't get in, I don't stand a chance."**

First things first. It had to be hard to be turned down by a school they loved, but did all that preparation really lead to nothing? Given everything these students had learned, the ways they had grown, and how they overcame adversity and embraced creativity in creating College Plans B, C, and Q, did they really get nothing out of it?

If so, they have every right to be unhappy, but not with the college. They should be unhappy watching the sun rise and set 1,307 times since the first day of ninth grade to the day the college said no, never once appreciating all that each of those days had to offer in and of themselves.

They should hang their heads a little to realize, just now, the difference they've made to their classmates, their teammates, and the people in the soup kitchen.

And if they look back with regret on the many times they blew off a compliment from a teacher or parent because the goal of college wasn't realized, that's more than OK. They now know that the goal of fully living each day was conquered with a flourish—and that understanding will make each day all the richer at the wonderful college that had the good sense (and room) to take them.

What about the colleges you applied to? They're looking for great students who have done wonderful things with their lives and will work nicely with the other admitted students. That blend goes beyond test score and class rank—it goes to who you are, what you care about, and how you see the world. Problem is, they run out of room before they run out of qualified applicants.

The thing to focus on then is not who told you no, but who told you yes. If a college wants you but runs out of room, that's their fault; if they don't see you for who you really are, well, maybe that's not the place for you after all. Either way, your contributions will be greatly admired, and badly needed, by the college that had the good sense to tell you yes, which means a no from any college simply cannot touch you.

CHAPTER 54

Three Kinds of Decisions

When you hear from a college, you'll get one of four decisions:

Admitted. Also known as the "thick" envelope, the mailed packet letting you know you're in typically includes information on housing, orientation, and financial aid. Be sure to read all of it; the information will be of great value to you if you need to decide among several offers of admission.

Conditional admission. Colleges offer you a seat in the freshman class with a requirement—generally, that you participate in a tutoring or student support program, that your first semester grades reach a certain level, or that you come to campus over the summer to participate in a college readiness program. These offers of admission are not an "either/ or" proposition—if you want to go to that college, you must satisfy the requirements outlined in the letter of admission.

Not offered admission. The news that a college cannot offer you admission usually comes in a thin envelope when it's mailed. Colleges mean it when they say they wish they could offer you admission, and they value your work as a student; it's just that they've run out of room. As I've said before, this isn't a judgment on your life; they just can't take everyone.

I'm sometimes asked if an admissions decision can be appealed. Just like every college handles admissions decisions differently, every college handles admissions appeals differently—and remember, colleges do not have to offer any kind of appeal at all. In general, follow these guidelines:

Read your letter closely. These letters often explain both the procedures you need to follow to file an appeal and the things colleges look for in an appeal. If your letter doesn't say anything about this, call the admissions office and ask what the appeals policy is—and remember, some colleges will not take appeals except in (or even in) very rare circumstances.

See if you can find out why you were denied admission in the first place. A discussion with a college admissions officer may give the college enough additional information about you to form the basis of an appeal. If the college needs more information, you can ask for details about what the college wants to see—or, in some cases, you can find out if an appeal would not be the best use of your time.

Generally speaking, colleges will look at an appeal closely if you can provide additional information above and beyond what you included in your original application—information that shows you are a strong and/or unique student. Marking period grades, progress reports from your current classes, additional letters of recommendation, a supporting paragraph or two from your counselor, previously unexplained circumstances—these kinds of things can make a difference (again, that's *can*).

Remember that a successful appeal depends on a variety of factors: your strength as a student, what you've been doing with your life since you applied, your continued interest in the college, the number of spaces the college has left to fill, you get the idea. In general, continued interest and strong grades may be able to get you in on appeal, but in some cases, it won't.

An appeal isn't a sure thing, and the extra energy it takes to put an appeal together—not just yours, but the energy of your counselor, your teachers, and the college—can be high at this time of year. Before you begin an appeal, be sure to think about your chances of success and your real interest in the college, and let your answers guide you accordingly.

That's three possible outcomes. Now, on to the fourth.

CHAPTER 55

Wait Lists

A letter indicating you've been wait-listed usually comes all by itself. The letter indicates the college is still considering your application but must hear from the admitted students before they may—again, that's may—offer you admission.

This is tricky for two reasons. First, it's tough to wait longer; you were ready to hear yes or no, and instead, you got "give us a little more time." Many students just can't live with not knowing anymore. If that's you, thank the college, say you're not interested, and move on.

Second, wait-list rules vary by college, so...

- Reread the letter from the college to see if it gives you any information about the wait list—how the order to making offers is determined, when it is determined, and what you need to do to stay on it. If all the admitted soccer players turn down College X and College Y, College X may only go to the wait list for soccer players, while College Y may start offering admission to the students at the top of a predetermined list, whether they play soccer or not. This makes for a pretty bad soccer team, but this does still happen at a few schools. Find out if you're dealing with an X or a Y.

- If this information isn't in the letter, call the college and ask. They may give you some suggestions on what to do; use them, since they are basically telling you how to improve your chances of getting off the list.

Next, it's decision time. Given the options you have, do you still feel you want to wait and hear back from this college? As you think about this, let these two questions be your guide:

1. If a slot doesn't open up at this college, what other college will I choose to go to?
2. If a slot does open up at this college, what college will I select?

If the answer to both questions is the same, you don't need the wait list. If your decision depends in part on financial aid, remember that the amount of aid that's available to students who come off the wait list is usually limited. Colleges typically offer all their aid to students who are admitted; as a result, the aid offered to students taken off the wait list is limited to the amount of aid turned down by admitted students. That's no reason to give up—it's just something to consider or ask about.

If you decide to go for it, don't be shy. "I want you to know I am still interested in attending College X this fall" sends a clear statement on where you stand; if this is your first-choice college, make sure you say that, as long as you mean it. Grades in current classes, additional awards, and maybe another letter of recommendation could make a difference, as long as the college lets you submit them. Send in one complete package of new material as soon as it's ready, and about two weeks later, call or email to let them know of your continued interest.

Most colleges won't review their wait list until after May 1, which is when most colleges want students to send in a deposit, or at least tell then they are coming. If you're still waiting to hear from a wait-listed college on April 30, put in the required deposit at another school, so you have somewhere to go in the fall. If the college of your dreams pulls you off the wait list later on, cancel your admission in writing at the other school—and know you probably won't get your deposit back.

If you want to go for it, give it your all—but remember, you already have a life; now you're just looking for a college.

CHAPTER 56

Waiting a Year

Tell me the truth; when I suggested you apply to six to ten schools when this all started, you thought I was crazy. Now, you're looking closely at your options, and you're not sure what to do.

It's right around now that many students think about putting college on hold. This happens a lot, and choosing to defer—right, the same word colleges use when they ask for more time with your application—has its advantages. Students who choose to defer often get the chance to do something they've always wanted to do—see the world, work with those in need, learn a language, earn even more money for college—or maybe just rest and recover.

Parents often freak out about this choice; they're afraid that once you're out of school, you won't go back. Colleges don't feel that way. In fact, most colleges let you take a year off and hold a spot for you for the following fall, as long as you ask for a deferral by May 1st of senior year and promise not to take classes at another school. Not every college does this, so be sure to ask your college if this is an option and what the requirements are.

If you think a deferral, or gap year, might be for you, apply to your colleges in your senior year as if you weren't going to defer. The logistics of applying to college after you graduate from high school can be huge. It's better to make a plan for next year while you're still in school, whether that plan includes college or not. No college is a good choice for many, as long as it's for a good reason, and as long as you have a plan.

"Fair enough," you think, "but where can I get some ideas about what else I could do?"

A number of websites can help you fill in the details on making a gap year. Some, such as Rustic Pathways and Where There Be Dragons, offer travel and study programs abroad, while other programs like Dynamy give students a chance to learn more about themselves and their world through internships. Make sure the company is credible, and look for student comments about the programs. Many of these programs can be pricey, and not all offer financial aid, so make sure you look into that as well.

Of course, you don't have to work with any specific program. Many faith-based groups offer students the chance to study English as a second language, and some students simply use the time to travel or work for a year. Whatever you end up doing is great, as long as it's planned ahead of time and your time has specific goals, made with the help and support of parents and others who know you well.

The last thing you want to do is think you're going to make up a plan as you go along. That may be your only option for a number of reasons (this happened a lot when COVID first hit), but if the main reason you're picking deferral is because you can't make up your mind about college, deferral is likely not the choice for you. Instead, you need to give serious thought to your future and what you need to do next year to bring those dreams to life.

CHAPTER 57

Still Can't Decide? Try This

As you make your way to a college choice, consider these ideas:

- Think college qualities, not college names. There are reasons you loved the colleges you applied to—the small class sizes, the classes they offered, the feel on campus. Write those qualities down, and see how each college measures up to them.
- Review your research on each college—one way or another. In a perfect world, spring of the senior year is the perfect time to visit each campus again. If that's just not an option, take another online tour (you'd be amazed what you see the second time).
- Debrief at the end. Once you're done with your list and your fact-finding, talk with your parents about what you saw. What's there that you like? What new questions do you have, and who can help answer those? Can you see yourself at this college?
- Seek parental input. It's great to show some independence, but your parents/guardians know you well. Invite their input. "Do you see me being happy there?"
- Compare the colleges you have, not the ones you wanted. Once you've reviewed the colleges, compare their strengths and

weaknesses, but make sure you're not thinking about the dream school that denied you. You may not find a perfect campus, but you'll most likely find a best one. Focus on that as your goal, and you'll be fine.

- Don't forget your heart. You might not be able to describe what makes a college right for you, but that's OK. You've done a lot of research and thinking so, at this point, you can trust your heart to lead you. Your head will remember why you felt this college was the right one once you get to campus in the fall.

- Think about what makes sense now. When you applied to all of these places last fall, you likely said, "If College X takes me, that's where I 'm going to go." There's no doubt you felt that way then, but that was seven months ago, and your interests and way of looking at the world may have changed since then. How you felt then is a factor for sure, but how you feel now is more important. Keep that in mind.

- Check finances one last time. If you have a college and it's a little out of reach, call the admissions office and the financial aid office—that's two separate calls—and tell them so. A sincere call shows them you're interested; not calling gives them no impression at all—and may leave you short in the wallet for no reason at all.

- Start the hunt again. If your choices really don't thrill you, wait until May 5th or so. That's when many colleges find they still have openings, and of course, they want to fill them. Getting financial aid might be a challenge, but you never know until you ask. The National Association for College Admission Counseling keeps an online list of colleges that are looking, but don't hesitate to call any college and ask about space.

- Wait. Many colleges you've applied to or expressed interest in may continue to send you emails and calls, even after you make your choice. In some cases, they will offer you some kind of incentive, such as financial aid or better housing, to get you to change your mind. These contacts can last for a long time—in some cases, even once you start college.

If any of these offers seem tempting, proceed with caution. Your first-choice college may not be perfect, but you likely know that college better than the colleges calling after May 1st to get you to go there. If you think a change makes sense, do your homework to make sure you know what you're getting into, and then notify your first college you aren't coming after all. You likely won't get your deposit back if there was one, but you can ask.

CHAPTER 58

The Final Exam of Choosing a College

Now that you've narrowed your choices, there are three final questions to ask:

Are you in love with what the college has to offer, or with what the college stands for? Once a college admits you, they will call you day and night, send you emails hourly, and text you in the middle of math class. Once, colleges even went so far as to send every admitted applicant a disposable cell phone, so the college knew they could get through to every student.

Some of this may be helpful—if you get a call from a student studying your major, great—but many of these communications are just designed to give you a feel or glow for the college that can cloud your judgment, not clear it. The same is true for financial aid packages. One student picked a school just because they gave him a $600 grant and called it an honors scholarship. That makes the school a little less expensive, but does it make it right for you?

The college you say yes to will be thrilled to have you, and that's important, but you won't be getting hourly texts once you hit campus, and the school mascot won't be escorting you to class every day. Classes, studying, and doing laundry will take up about 150 of your college days every year, while home football games will take up about six. This is your new home—make sure your choice about that home is on a solid foundation.

Should you start locally and transfer? If money is tight, consider starting at a local community college or four-year institution where you can commute, live at home for a while, and then transfer to your dream school to finish. You'll have to work very closely every semester with an adviser *at the college you are transferring to,* to make sure your classes will transfer for the degree you want, but if this means less stress, less loans, and more of a chance to afford your final two years at the place you really want to be, it's worth considering.

It's time to deposit, and you just can't decide between your schools. Is it OK to deposit at more than one school at a time? No.

For most schools, May 1st is the time you have to tell one—and only one—school that you are coming. They need this information to plan, and that takes time.

Consider this. You decide to enroll at a college that has small classes, which you really like. You head to class on the first day, only to discover that thirty students double deposited—they told more than one school they'd be going there in the fall. All thirty of these students decided not to come to your college, and they just told the college the day before. It's too late for the college to go to their wait list, so those seats are now empty, and so is their budget. They cancel classes, lay off teachers they suddenly can't afford, and put students in classes of one hundred. So much for the education you had hoped for.

Telling lots of schools yes with a deposit is like saying yes to ten prom dates—you might get more time to choose, but it hurts lots of people in the process, including you. Students stay on wait lists for no reason, colleges schedule classes that won't have enough students, and parents lose deposits that could go toward textbooks—or retirement.

It's great to have options, but the band is playing, and it's time to dance. Size up your partners, pick the one that will get you across the dance floor with the right balance of support and excitement, and move to the music of the future—your future.

CHAPTER 59

What Really Got You In, and What Really Will Keep You Out

Now that you've selected a college, you're probably involved in very serious academic pursuits like planning senior skip day and planting a whoopee cushion on the principal's chair during graduation, so I'll quickly address two issues.

First, congratulations on your acceptance into college. Your college admission letter is an affirmation of the hard work you put in, the risks you took in high school, and the many contributions you made outside the classroom.

This is worth thinking about because many students thank teachers or counselors for "getting them in" college. I think I know what you mean when you say that, but I'm not sure you do.

Too many media outlets try to make the college application process more "interesting" by shaping it like a TV reality show (*Survivor—Showdown in the Dining Hall*). This explains why your parents may have given you SAT flash cards for your sixth birthday or a gold bracelet at age thirteen with the Common Application's website inscribed on it. It also explains why your mother's therapist can send her daughter to Cornell without taking out any loans.

Thanks to these shows, college counselors are seen as wizards, the Dumbledores of college access who bring you into their office just to get a sense of your aura. Later, when they sense the Force is with them, they call the college of your choice on a special red phone, whisper the incantation *Student Acceptus* into the phone, and voila! You're in!

Of course, we make you jump through the hoops of getting good grades, working hard outside of school, and writing several drafts of essays designed to communicate your understanding of yourself and the world around you—but this is window dressing. The real work happens in our offices when the moon is but a thin crescent in the northern sky and the wind blows toward Harvard Yard, Touchdown Jesus, or the statue of Sparty.

The world would have you believe this, but it isn't true. Yes, we help you find the right mix of challenge, opportunity, and growth at your next school. We also help give colleges a complete understanding of your life through the right mix of letters of recommendation, essays, and interviews.

Still, we are not the ones who "get you in." You earn the grades, write the essays, and make it happen. That's as it should be, since it's not only who you are and what you do that gets you into school but it keeps you there as well.

And that's my second point. Colleges care a little more about your last semester grades than you think. It's great that you have college in sight, and there are lots of things you want to do senior year to say goodbye to high school with a flourish. But if you slack off now, the colleges have the right to decide maybe learning doesn't matter to you after all, which means there's no point in admitting you after all.

If you need help remembering what exactly you were studying before senioritis struck, you may want to track down Dumbledore and borrow his Pensieve. Just remember, school counselors ain't Dumbledore— they honestly told the colleges you would be a great student, and they'll honestly have to tell the college they've changed their mind if you give them reason to do so.

So how about you forget about the whoopee for now and focus on the cushion?

CHAPTER 60

Before You Go to College

Once graduated, here are some recommendations on how to spend part of your summer. College is about trying new things, and even if some of them may seem to have been around awhile, they're still new to you and have something to show you. Give these a spin, and you'll be more flexible than Gumby after a yoga class:

Movie you must see before you go to college. *The Shawshank Redemption* was overlooked when it was released the same year as *Forrest Gump*. Now it's on cable every month. A story about forgiveness, second chances, and negotiating with the world, this isn't an easy film to watch, but it talks about hope, determination, and always doing what's right. It will give you the skills to manage Intro to Econ, eccentric roommates, and more.

Movie clip you must see before you go to college. Call it cheesy, but the first scene in *The Sound of Music* (do an online search for "Sound of Music opening") is worth the two minutes and twenty-two seconds it will occupy your life. All you see are the mountains of Austria, and all you hear is the magnificent voice of a young Julie Andrews. Success in college demands the ability to stop and appreciate that which is simple and beautiful. Watching this clip will also help you understand why your father's (or grandfather's) adolescence was complicated by having an intense crush on a nun.

Song you must listen to before you go to college. The second movement of Mozart's Concerto for Flute and Harp ("Rampal Mozart Flute & Harp Concerto in C major"—YouTube) is the finest piece Mozart wrote, and its full potential was realized by Jean-Pierre Rampal and Lilly Laskine. Rampal started out as a premed major, but his heart had other designs, and he went on to become the premiere flutist of all time. This is a perfect piece to begin your discovery of "classical" music. Just remember, anyone who tells you all of Mozart's music is the same has no idea what they're talking about, and no idea how to listen. Keep that in mind.

Song clip you must watch before you go to college. It took less than two minutes for Ella Fitzgerald and the Manhattan Transfer to find their place in Grammy history with their rendition of *How High the Moon* ("Ella Manhattan How High"). Your goal in college is to work this hard to make everything look this easy—and if you leave college without an appreciation for good jazz, your tuition was wasted.

Phrase you must add to your vocabulary. "Absolutely." Colleges are run by administrative assistants—veteran, organized professionals who have a way of doing things that is older than Stonehenge. This method almost always works to your advantage, except at peak times when every student needs help, and their system of order is on the brink of collapse. This is where you come in.

You: "I need to drop a class."

Administrative assistant, peering over glasses: "Have you seen your adviser?"

You: "Absolutely."

You have restored some sense of order to their universe, and they will never, ever forget you. That's good. Trust me.

Phrase you must delete from your vocabulary. "No problem." One of these assistants may thank you for doing something. The only way to get off their good side is to respond with anything other than "you're welcome." Practice now.

Book you must read before you go to college. *How the Irish Saved Civilization* by Thomas Cahill. Neither fiction nor a scholarly work, it's like your Irish neighbor telling you the true but enhanced story of the vital role Irish monks played in restoring education in Europe in the time of Saint Patrick. You won't read anything this easy or biased in college, but it's the story of how modest people engaged in diligent efforts can change history.

Congratulations.

CHAPTER 61

Once You're There

What you do and choose not to do during the first two months of college is crucial to the rest of your freshman year, and finishing college in general. If there are any chapters in this book I hope you scan into your phone, it's this one and the next one.

Set up a regular study routine. No matter what schedule you had in high school, college is going to be different, mostly because you will find yourself with incredibly open periods of time during, say, Tuesday morning or Thursday afternoon.

The key is to put together a study schedule. Every college class is designed for you to make the most of it by studying, note-taking, and writing for two hours outside of class, for every hour you are in class. Book it now. It may vary a little from week to week, so part of Sunday is always about reviewing and updating the schedule. But it can be more consistent than you think. Stick with it.

Don't study in your room. Studying in a library may be a new idea to you, but so is free time on Tuesdays. There's a good chance the library offers tours on how to make the most of the library. Sounds silly, but take the tour, and see if a veteran student can offer you their insights.

Use the help that's offered. Colleges have writing centers, math centers, and study centers for one reason: this isn't grade thirteen. College is a different animal from high school, so just like twelfth grade was harder than ninth grade, college is harder than high school. Utilize the expertise of the helpers.

This is especially true for your instructors. Colleges require them to have office hours, certain times each week when they hang out in their offices, hoping students come by to ask questions, share ideas, and just say hello.

Here's the thing: no one does this. Except for the first day of class and the week of any test, your professors spend their office hours reading golf magazines. This is your chance to bring your serious questions and ideas to an expert, or to simply ask them how you should go about studying for their class. (Note that this is different from asking, "What's going to be on the test?" Generally, that's a no-no.) Make the most of your college experience. Get the experts to help you.

This includes the mental health services on campus. Colleges are seeing an increase in the number of students who need help making sense of the demands of college and life. This means there are more resources out there than ever before to help you. It also means you aren't alone in feeling this way. These programs are confidential and usually free. They also are very freeing. You deserve that.

Get a real bank account. Some students have had their own account for years, and others haven't. Either way, you're now in a place where it's much easier, and too easy, to spend five dollars on coffee every day.

Make sure you have an account that's updated daily, so you can look at it at least three times a week. All that coffee adds up, and if there's no money left for books, that's going to be a problem.

Think twice about getting a credit card. The offers are everywhere— the bookstore, the student center, the coffee shop—to get a credit card. They are certainly nice to have in emergencies, but they can easily become a distraction if you charge those five-dollar coffees and then don't pay off the credit card completely every month. Your bank account likely has some kind of automatic loan attached to it when you run out of money. Set your account up so that you get a text when it kicks in. With a little practice, this will meet your needs nicely. If you must have a credit card, talk with your parents about sharing theirs. The terms of their card will be much friendlier than the offers you'll get on campus.

Volunteer in the community. One way college is the same as high school is how it needs volunteers to make things go. From call centers to helplines to food drives, colleges—and the towns they're in—are better places when people choose to make them better, and you are one of those people. The YMCA, the elementary school, the Kiwanis club—they need you, and there's a part of you that needs to be discovered by you in helping them. Don't pass up this learning activity.

Touch base with home at least once a week. It's best to schedule this as part of your study time, the same time every week. They love you. This matters.

CHAPTER 62

In Case

Sometimes the life you build turns out to be the life you don't want to live after all. If that happens to you, I offer you this story for safekeeping. I hope this lad's adventures do not await you, but in the event a day comes that leaves you wondering about your own capabilities, remember this.

My first client was a wreck. He was a bright enough boy, with good grades and test scores to boot, but no self-esteem. None. He clung to the sides of the hallways between classes, didn't ask many questions about college, and ended up in the honors college of a public university he had no business going to. For as nice as it was for some, he had other things to do, and just didn't know it.

Fall of freshman year, disaster was right at his heels. Between the blasting stereos and the late-night screaming—and this was in the honors dorm—he finally figured out this wasn't the place for him. After two weeks, he packed his bags and headed for home. He managed to enroll in the fall semester of a local commuter college that started late, but he really longed for something different. He reapplied to a residential college where he thought things might be better. He knew some students who went there, the campus was pretty, and it was big enough for him to be anonymous, just like always.

He headed out for his third college on New Year's Day, less than six months after he'd graduated from high school. After about three weeks, it was pretty clear this place wasn't heaven either, and yet, something was different. The stereos weren't as loud—it was winter semester, after all—and a couple professors talked to him like he was a human being, so he decided this was the place to make his stand. For once, he was gong to steer his destiny and not the other way around.

With that change in attitude, things worked out pretty well. He met up with some high school friends, who invited him to join their intramural basketball and softball teams (he was awful, but it didn't matter—so were they). His understanding of classical music impressed a couple of girls enough to get past his low self-esteem and go out on a couple of dates—nothing intense, but still reassuring.

His academic interests led him to work as an assistant on a research project studying language development among American children—groundbreaking stuff at the time—and he gained the respect of his instructors, especially the writing profs, who told him he really had something if he wanted to work at it.

Twenty-four months after starting at his third college—two and a half years after graduating from high school—he signed his first employment contract. Two days after that, he walked across the commencement stage, not once but twice, having earned enough credits for two separate degrees, making him the first in his family to graduate from college, and a working stiff to boot.

Three months after that, he turned twenty.

I know you have worked hard to build the very best future you possibly can. In the event your current plan doesn't work out, there will be another plan for another day. Listen closely, always be receptive to the possible, ask for help when you need it, and take help when it is offered. Know that the choice to succeed is ultimately yours to make and yours alone, but also know you are never alone.

Onward.

CHAPTER 63

What's Next

No book is perfect, and that's certainly true for this one. There is more to say and more to think about, but it's probably best if that "more" comes from discussions with colleges, counselors, teachers, and parents. If this book has done its job, you now know that a college choice isn't about rocket science, tea leaves, or the only twenty-five colleges newspapers spend way too much time talking about.

It's about you. Colleges want to know what you've done in the world, how you see the world, and what you think about tomorrow. Get that into a college application, and you'll get into that college with ease. Better than that, you'll have the skills you need to live a rich, full life—and that's what college is all about.

It's also important to remember that a keystone of rich, full lives is making wise decisions, a skill you'll need to put into practice not only with your college decisions, but also in the classroom—and out. As you celebrate senior year, there's a good chance you'll be hanging out at parties that are wide open. This is even truer once you get to college, where there will be no bells to remind you about what you need to do or when you need to do it. That means the choices are pretty much up to you.

I don't want to turn this into a health class; instead, just let me remind you of some things you probably already know.

- Developmentally, you aren't through growing yet, and the fine tuning your body is doing requires as few pollutants as possible. In addition, many of you may still be in a developmental phase where drugs and alcohol create a dependency that's difficult to shake, not just now but forever. So yes, being eighteen or nineteen or twenty is very different from being twenty-one.
- The later it gets at night, the more likely it is that the person driving the car next to you is drunk. It's an old statistic, but I once read that one out of every three drivers on the road after 11:00 p.m. on weekends is legally drunk.
- Legally, drunk driving, possession of alcohol by a minor, furnishing of alcohol to a minor, and sale of illegal drugs to anyone are all crimes. If convicted, this can be devastating to both your life and your college plans, as well as applications for loans, employment, military service—and lives beyond your own.

As a counselor, part of my job is to help you create the best possible future. Keeping that goal in mind, now and forever…

- Do not, under any circumstance, get into a car driven by a drunk driver (any drunk driver) or where alcohol or drugs are being used. Both are unsafe. With the latter, you'll go to jail; with the former, you could end up hurt, or worse.
- If you're driving past 11:00 p.m. on any night, plan a route home that takes you past as few restaurants and bars as possible.

- If offered a substance that is unsafe, illegal, or unwise for you to have, graciously say no. If it's impossible to be gracious, it's time to lose that friend, move on, and head home.

Blind obedience to laws is questionable, for sure—life teaches us all that. But obedience to a law you may not fully understand is a different thing. You've worked hard to build a bright life, so do yourself and the world a favor and stick around to live it out. I promise one day the laws you may not fully understand will make stone-cold-sober perfect sense.

Wow. That sounded just like a counselor. Guess I'm busted.

Don't you be.

CHAPTER 64

Six Words for Parents

Supporting your child in the college selection process is one of the most important things parents can do. It also seems to be one of the most mysterious, since applying to college has changed so much in a generation. If only the colleges had advice for parents to follow.

It turns out they do. I ask colleges all the time for advice to parents on how to help their child with this exciting opportunity. Every college—every single one—offers this advice:

"Let your child drive the bus."

This advice, combined with long-standing conventional wisdom, gets to the heart of the college application process and shows what admissions officers are looking for in a successful applicant beyond the numbers:

Initiative. From start to finish, a college application has to send the message that applying to this school was the student's idea, and the student is excited enough to do something to bring that idea to life.

This is why so many colleges want students to visit campus or meet the admissions representative at a local college fair; it shows the student is serious about their application. That seriousness is questioned when any part of the application—especially the essays—is completed by an adult, or when parents call the admissions office to ask questions. This is particularly true if the parent starts the call by saying, "We're applying to your college next year." If the student wants to start building a meaningful relationship with the college, they make the calls, complete all parts of the application, and speak in first person.

Synthesis. Well-meaning parents insist they only help their child complete a college application because it is too complicated. Colleges certainly don't want the process to discourage students; at the same time, applicants show they possess the traits needed to be successful students at selective colleges by demonstrating the flexibility, organization, and persistence needed to create an application crafted exclusively by the student. That's why it's best for students to schedule an hour or two each weekend in the fall to focus on college applications. It gives them the best chance to create an application that is rich with their voice, and their voice alone. Counselors and teachers can be of help, and your moral support makes all the difference. But the work is theirs to do.

Originality. Everyone has a unique view of the world, and a good college application gives the admissions office a glimpse into a student's ability to share their particular vantage point. Colleges understand that view may not be fully developed at age seventeen—in fact, most hope it isn't—but they also understand that unique view should be consistent across all parts of the application. A twenty-minute weekly meeting (see chapter 12) between parents and applicant gives the student the right mix of structure and encouragement to shape their own answers, and assure their ownership of the application process.

Authenticity. Students have different reasons for attending college, but each reason has a common purpose: students want to get something out of the experience. A strong college application shows the admissions office what that purpose is, and taking the time to wrestle with each part of a college application not only gives the application more clarity and confidence, but it also gives the applicant more clarity and confidence.

It may be hard for parents to watch students struggle at first with this important task, just as it wasn't easy to watch them strike out at the plate, listen to their first violin solo, or feel them let the clutch out too soon. Great hitters and virtuosos are made with time, effort, and the opportunity to get better, and so are good drivers. The best way to help them reach their college destination is to give them the keys.

About the Author

Patrick O'Connor is college counselor, chief strategist and CEO of College is Yours, an organization focused on improving college opportunity and success for all students. Born and raised in Detroit, he has been a college counselor since 1984, serving students and families from all walks of life, both in high schools and community college. In addition to writing a weekly column for *High School Counselor Week*, his writing has appeared in the *Washington Post*, the *Christian Science Monitor*, the *Detroit Free Press*, the *Detroit News*, *Admissions Intel*, and *Inside Higher Ed*.

Patrick has served as president of the National Association for College Admission Counseling (NACAC) and the Michigan Association for College Admission Counseling (MACAC). He is a past board chair of the Michigan College Access Network and served as the Inaugural School Counselor Ambassador Fellow with the US Department of Education. He is a recipient of the Outstanding Faculty Award from Oakland Community College, where he is a member of the political science faculty. He has also received the Margaret Addis Service to NACAC Award, the NACAC Government Relations Award, and the

William Gramenz Award (for outstanding service to college counseling in Michigan). He holds five college degrees and is the first in his family to graduate from college.

Patrick has worked with thousands of counselors, providing professional development and training in college counseling. He is the author of the highly acclaimed *College Counseling for School Counselors* and teaches one of the few courses in college counseling available in the country. He played a key role in groundbreaking legislation to make sure Michigan school counselors have the latest training in college counseling, and he teaches a number of online professional development courses in college counseling. It is estimated that Patrick's work, directly with families or with school counselors, has allowed him to affect the college choices of over one million students in his career.

Patrick lives in suburban Detroit and can be reached through www.collegeisyours.com.

CPSIA information can be obtained
at www.ICGtesting.com
Printed in the USA
LVHW091522090821
694908LV00005B/116